Battling MALARIA

ON THE FRONT LINES AGAINST A GLOBAL KILLER

Connie Goldsmith

Twenty-First Century Books · Minneapolis

To the Bill and Melinda Gates Foundation, for its extraordinary generosity in the fight against malaria; and to the thousands of doctors, nurses, and other health-care workers who give their time and experience to fight malaria and other diseases of poverty around the world

Twenty-First Century Books
A division of Lerner Publishing Group, Inc.
241 First Avenue North
Minneapolis, MN 55401 U.S.A.

Website address: www.lernerbooks.com

Library of Congress Cataloging-in-Publication Data

Goldsmith, Connie, 1945–
    Battling malaria : on the front lines against a global killer / by Connie Goldsmith.
        p.   cm.
    Includes bibliographical references and index.
    ISBN: 978–0–8225–8580–0 (lib. bdg. : alk. paper)
    1. Malaria—Juvenile literature. I. Title.
  RC157.G65 2011
  616.9'362—dc22   2009020324

Manufactured in the United States of America
1 – DP – 7/15/10

TABLE OF CONTENTS

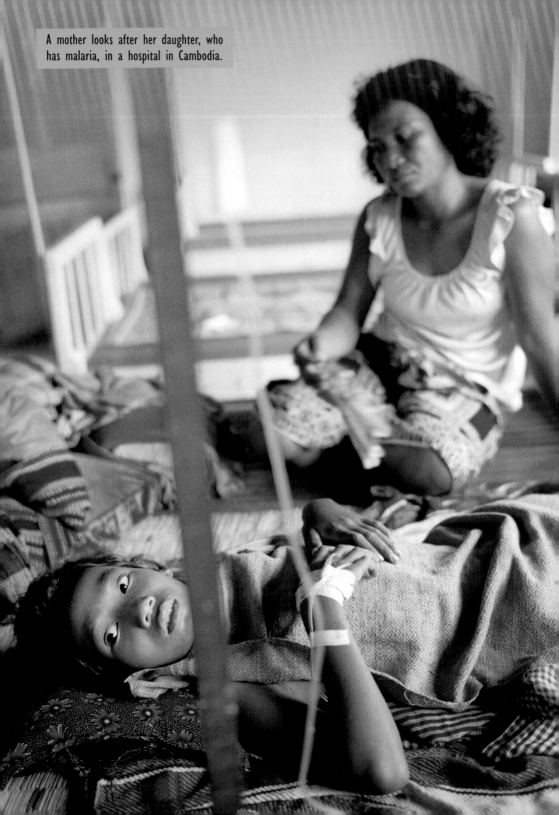

A mother looks after her daughter, who has malaria, in a hospital in Cambodia.

A MAJOR GLOBAL KILLER

U.S. physician Terrence Smith has worked in medical clinics in Thailand and Myanmar (also called Burma) in Southeast Asia. He describes a scene that is typical in these and many other nations around the world. "Mothers carry their children through the forest to the clinic in their arms or wrapped in a shawl on their backs," Smith says. "The children have malaria, and they are too weak to cry, too weak even to swat the flies away from their faces. The children don't complain when they are in pain. The mothers are stoic and don't complain either, even when they fear their children will die. Malaria is so common that it goes untreated. . . . Mothers usually don't bring their children into the clinic until the child is very sick and suffering the complications of severe malaria, such as seizures or unconsciousness."

If the World Health Organization (WHO; an agency of the United Nations) had a most wanted list of dreaded diseases, malaria would make the top three, along with HIV/AIDS and tuberculosis. Malaria sickens between three hundred million and five hundred million people around the world each year. That's more than the combined population of the United States and Canada.

Not only does malaria make a lot of people sick, it's a major global killer. More than one million people die from malaria each year. In Africa one child dies of malaria every thirty seconds. On the day you read this chapter, malaria will kill three thousand people. Most of them will be young children.

Malaria is caused by a tiny parasite. A parasite is an organism that lives in or on another organism known as the host. As they feed and reproduce, parasites often make their hosts sick. The malaria parasite spends part of its life cycle in humans and part in mosquitoes. The parasite needs both humans and mosquitoes to survive. People do

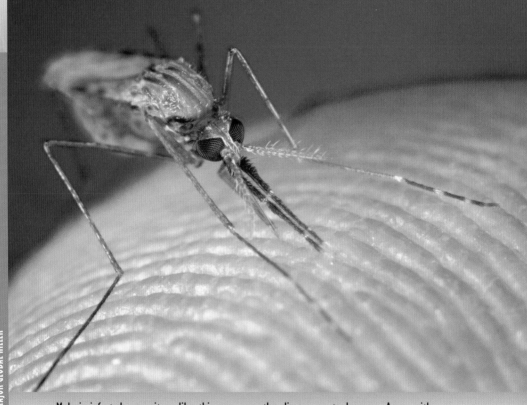

Malaria-infected mosquitoes like this one pass the disease on to humans. Areas with warm, wet weather have more mosquitoes and therefore more malaria.

not usually catch malaria from one another. In most cases, malaria passes from person to person by the bite of infected mosquitoes.

Malaria has been sickening and killing people for thousands of years. In the mid-twentieth century, WHO and other groups made great strides in wiping out the disease. They conquered malaria in some places and sharply curbed it in others.

The victory was short-lived, however. In the late twentieth century, malaria stormed back in much of the world. Not only has malaria returned to some areas, it is also spreading to new areas. The disease has become more dangerous as well. It sickens more people than ever before and makes people sicker than in the past.

About half the world's people live in malaria-stricken countries. Many of these countries are among the poorest in the world. Countries cannot thrive when their citizens live with constant illness and poverty. Around the world, scientists, health workers, governments, and private organizations are working to prevent malaria, lessen its spread, and better treat people who get the disease. If we can control malaria, millions of people around the world will enjoy healthier lives.

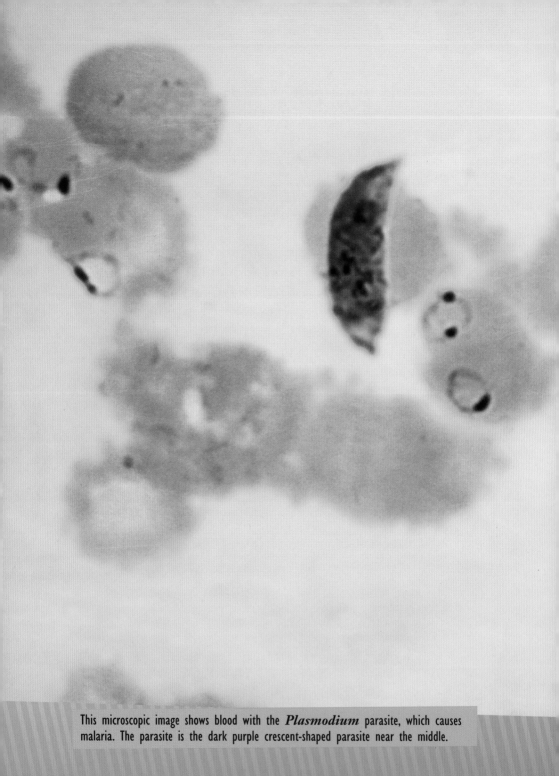

This microscopic image shows blood with the *Plasmodium* parasite, which causes malaria. The parasite is the dark purple crescent-shaped parasite near the middle.

Chapter 1

MALARIA THROUGH THE AGES

Malaria is an ancient disease. In 2002 scientists at the U.S. National Institutes of Health determined that *Plasmodium*, the malaria parasite, has been around for at least one hundred thousand years. The parasite is much older than previously thought and more complex than ever imagined.

Some scientists believe that *Plasmodium* originally infected birds. It probably spread to humans thousands of years ago, when people in Africa began raising birds such as chickens and ducks. *Plasmodium* might have moved from birds to people when someone slaughtered an infected chicken for the dinner pot. Then the chicken's contaminated blood entered an open wound on the cook's hand. Since then malaria has tormented and killed billions of people. It has even changed the course of world history.

It's Ancient History

Thousands of years ago, ancient people wrote about malaria. In about 2550 B.C., Chinese emperor Huang Ti wrote about the disease in a book called *Nei Ching*. Some doctors consider it to be the world's oldest medical book.

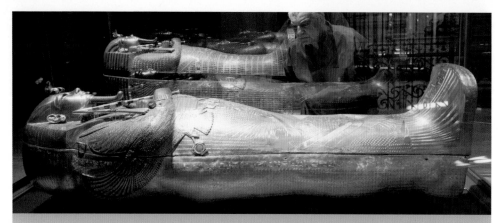

In 2010 scientists discovered that Tutankhamen, a king of ancient Egypt, most likely died of malaria. After death, King Tut was mummified and placed in an ornate coffin.

Around 1325 B.C., the ancient Egyptians wrote about malaria, or swamp fever as they called it, in a book of magical remedies and spells. The book, later called the *London Medical Papyrus*, was written in hieroglyphics, the ancient Egyptian system of picture writing. Modern scientists have found evidence of malaria in Egyptian mummies. The people whose bodies were made into mummies probably died of the disease.

In the 500s B.C., in ancient India, a surgeon named Sushruta wrote a medical book called *Sushruta Samhita*. In it he described the symptoms of malaria and its cycle of fevers and chills. He correctly blamed malaria on the bite of "certain insects," a fact lost to science until the late 1800s.

About one hundred years after *Sushruta*, the ancient Greek physician Hippocrates described malaria in detail. Hippocrates wrote of three kinds of malaria, differentiated by their cycles of chills and fevers. Most people of Hippocrates' time thought that illness was a sign of unhappy gods or of evil spirits. But Hippocrates disagreed. He believed that weather, dirty drinking water, or a person's own poor health and weakness could lead to malaria and many other illnesses.

Some ancient Greek writings told of malaria wiping out entire rural populations. Historians believe that malaria played a role in the decline of Greek city-states such as Athens and Sparta. The disease weakened people, leaving them unable to fight off invading armies.

Ancient healers used a variety of treatments for malaria, including magic spells and charms. Egyptian healers probably bathed feverish malaria sufferers in fresh urine, a common treatment for fevers at the time. The ancient Chinese discovered the first effective treatment for malaria. It was the qinghao plant. During the second century B.C., the Chinese wrote about the plant in a medical text called *52 Remedies*. The plant's healing power was probably unknown outside China at the time.

"Bad Air"

It fell to the ancient Romans, based in Italy, to give malaria its modern name. Until recent times, marshes and swamplands covered vast sections of Italy. Rome, Italy's capital, was said to have more malaria than any other big city on Earth. At first called Roman fever, or marsh fever, the illness returned with a vengeance each summer after the yearly flooding of the Tiber River. As the river receded, it left pools of stagnant (still) water behind.

Stagnant water provides perfect breeding grounds for the *Anopheles* mosquito—the mosquito that carries the human malaria parasite. But the ancient Romans didn't know that mosquitoes carry malaria. The Romans thought the disease came from stinky gases—caused by rotting plants and dead animals—that arose from swamps and drifted into villages and towns. The Romans called these gases *mala aria*, or "bad air." That's how marsh fever became known as malaria.

A Roman named Marcus Terentius Varro, who lived in the first century B.C., came tantalizingly close to recognizing the true nature of malaria. He believed the "bad air" around Rome teemed with *animaletti*, or "little animals." He said they were "minute [tiny] animals, invisible to the eye, that breed in the swamps, and borne by the air, reach inside of the body by way of the mouth and nose, and cause disease." Centuries later, scientists proved Varro right when they discovered the *Plasmodium* parasite.

Even though malaria sickened many Roman citizens, it sometimes helped protect Rome from attack. On some occasions, by the time invaders reached the city, many had fallen ill with the disease. Ultimately, malaria took a

Malaria was widespread in ancient Rome. Romans thought that "bad air" caused the disease.

heavy toll on Italy. The once-mighty Roman Empire fell to invaders around A.D. 476. Many historians believe that malaria, which weakened Rome's soldiers and civilians alike, contributed to the collapse.

The Fever Tree

For most of human history, malaria affected only the continents of Europe, Africa, and Asia. The malaria parasite was not present in either the people or the mosquitoes of North, Central, and South America. Historians believe that early European explorers and soldiers brought the malaria parasite within their bodies to the Americas in the 1500s and 1600s. Local mosquitoes fed on the newcomers, and then the mosquitoes carried the parasite to indigenous (local) peoples.

WHAT IT'S LIKE TO HAVE MALARIA

In 2007 journalist Coumba Makalou got malaria while working in her home country of Mali. She describes the disease at its worst:

> I awoke to what felt like lightning going through my legs, and then spreading through my body and in my head. Probably the worst headache, body aches, and chills you could possibly imagine. It felt like I was being stung repeatedly by an electric shock gun and could barely control my movements. The pain was so intense; I actually believed I was dying, literally crying out in pain so bad that I was taken to a 24 hour clinic that night at 3 A.M.

However, long before malaria appeared in their lands, the native peoples of Peru and Ecuador in South America used the bark of a tree to treat fevers caused by other diseases. The red-barked tree, known in modern times as the *Cinchona* tree, grew in the high foothills of the Andes Mountains.

In the 1600s, European priests traveled to South America, intent on educating the people there and converting them to Christianity. The priests built churches, schools, medical clinics, and apothecaries (pharmacies). Local people told the priests about tree bark that could cure fevers. They gave the priests samples of the miracle bark. Ground into a bitter-tasting powder and dissolved in hot water, the bark controlled fevers effectively. Priests promptly added the bark to their apothecaries.

One of the priests in Peru wondered if *Cinchona* bark would help treat the malaria that regularly ravaged Italy. The priest took a sample of the bark from an apothecary in Lima, Peru. He carried it to Italy in 1632. The bark proved an instant success. Not only did it stop chills and fever but it also cured most people of their malaria. Overwhelming demand for the bark of the "fever tree" swept first through Italy and then across the rest of Europe.

Using the fastest sailing vessels of the time, merchants shipped the bark across the Atlantic Ocean to Europe, where it sold for a fortune. Expeditions sailed from Europe to South America to bring back seeds and saplings of the fever tree. But these efforts failed. The young trees died along the way, long before they reached Europe. And the seeds of *Cinchona* trees did not grow well in Europe. For two hundred years, South America was the only place to get *Cinchona* bark.

In addition to exploring and settling the Americas, Europeans took over territories in Africa and Asia. They built cities and opened mines, farms, and other businesses. Around 1850 Europeans finally succeeded in growing *Cinchona* trees on farms in India, Java, and Sri Lanka in southern Asia. By then the medication from the tree was called quinine. People made quinine from the tree's bark, branches, and roots. It proved effective in preventing as well as treating malaria.

Not So Long Ago

In the mid-1800s, scientists and doctors still didn't know much about malaria. They suspected it was caused by tiny organisms called bacteria. These organisms cause many diseases, such as gonorrhea, Lyme disease, strep throat, tuberculosis, and whooping cough. Malaria was a complex puzzle that took scientists many decades to solve. Three names—Laveran, Golgi, and Ross—are forever linked to the puzzle's solution.

French surgeon Charles-Louis-Alphonse Laveran

Charles-Louis-Alphonse Laveran was a French army surgeon in the late 1800s. While working in North Africa, in French-ruled Algeria, he searched without success for a malaria-causing organism in air and water. He then turned his attention to blood. Using a microscope, Laveran was the first person to see malaria parasites in blood. The creatures appeared as round bodies both inside and outside of red blood cells. Laveran noticed that the malaria parasite looked different at different points in its life cycle. He published his findings, "New Parasite Found in the Blood of Several Patients Suffering from Marsh Fever," in a medical journal in 1880.

In 1886 Italian scientist Camillo Golgi identified two different forms of malaria. In one form, the patient had a fever every other day. In the second form, the patient had a fever every third day. Golgi also observed that the fever coincided with the movement of the parasite from the patient's liver into the bloodstream. After Golgi's discoveries, between 1890 and 1897, other Italian and U.S. researchers identified and named the four different species (kinds) of the *Plasmodium* parasite that cause human malaria.

The last piece of the puzzle slipped into place in 1897. By then scientists had identified the parasite in human blood and learned much about it. But no one yet knew how people got infected. Did they breathe in the parasite? Did they eat it in contaminated food or drink it in dirty water?

Italian scientist Camillo Golgi *(above)* and British physician Ronald Ross *(below)*

British physician Ronald Ross discovered the answers. Ross dissected an *Anopheles* mosquito after it had fed on the blood of a patient with malaria. Ross found the *Plasmodium* parasite in the mosquito's stomach. Clearly, the parasite spent stages of its life in both mosquitoes and people. People got the disease from being bitten by infected mosquitoes. Mosquitoes got the disease from biting infected people.

Ross said, "Malarial fever is important not only because of the misery it inflicts upon mankind, but also because of the serious opposition it has always given to the march of civilization. No wild deserts . . . no geographical difficulties have proven so inimical [hostile] to civilization as this disease."

In the early twentieth century, the scientific community honored the three pioneers for their contributions to malaria research. Ross's work won him a Nobel Prize in 1902. Golgi received a Nobel Prize in 1906, and Laveran won a Nobel Prize in 1907.

Mosquitoes and the Panama Canal

Scientists finally knew that a parasite caused malaria and that the parasite spread from person to person by mosquitoes. The next step was to figure out how to stop the spread of the disease. The first big battle between people and mosquitoes took place in a 42-mile-wide (68-kilometer-wide) piece of real estate known as the Isthmus of Panama.

Panama is a small and narrow nation in Central America. The Atlantic Ocean lies to the north of Panama, and the Pacific Ocean lies to the south. Since the 1500s, Europeans had dreamed of building a canal across Panama. This way, a boat traveling between the Atlantic and Pacific oceans could cut through Panama rather than sail around the tip of South America. This shortcut would save thousands of miles and many weeks of travel.

However, the mosquito thwarted that dream for nearly four hundred years. The dense tropical jungle of Panama, with its nine-month rainy season and high temperatures, provided the perfect breeding ground for mosquitoes. The local mosquitoes carried both malaria and a deadly disease called yellow fever.

After successfully completing the Suez Canal in Egypt in 1869, a group of French builders tried to cut a canal through the disease-infested jungle of Panama. This team started work on the Panama Canal in 1882. But because of rampant disease and the brutal tropical climate, thousands of construction workers died and the attempt failed. The project ended in financial ruin in 1888. The mosquitoes had won the first round.

Over the next decade, jungle grew over the abandoned French construction site. Meanwhile, the United States arranged to build the canal. The U.S. team started work in 1904. At the time, it was the largest construction project ever undertaken. Completion of the canal was vital to the expansion of world travel and trade.

The workforce struggled to dig through the jungle and over a mountain. But malaria and yellow fever sickened and killed many workers. During the first two years of construction, twenty-six thousand men worked on the canal. More than twenty-one thousand of them went to the hospital for malaria at some point during their work. Several hundred men died of malaria.

A group of U.S. military doctors and engineers, led by Colonel William Gorgas, made a plan to eliminate malaria in the region. To control mosquitoes, workers drained pools of standing water around houses and villages. In ponds and swamps that could not be drained, workers sprayed petroleum-based oil to kill mosquito larvae (newly hatched mosquitoes that floated on the water's surface). They used chemical insecticides to kill larvae when oiling the water

A worker sprays oil in a swamp in Panama in the early 1900s to kill mosquito larvae.

didn't work. Workers put screens on the windows and doors of government buildings and the sleeping quarters to keep out mosquitoes. To both prevent and treat malaria, they gave free quinine tablets to the construction workers. Finally, they collected mosquitoes for study.

The mosquito control plan was a success. By the end of the project, about fifty thousand men were working on the canal, but fewer than six thousand had gone to the hospital for malaria. Malaria in both canal workers and the local population had dropped dramatically. Yellow fever had been totally eradicated (wiped out) around the canal.

The Panama Canal was completed in 1914, after ten years of work. Nearly one hundred years later, the canal is still important to world trade. About fourteen thousand ships pass through the canal each year.

Malaria in the United States

Malaria was no stranger to North America. "Fever and ague," as it was sometimes called, took a heavy toll on European settlers and early U.S. leaders. Historians believe that presidents George Washington, Abraham Lincoln, and Ulysses Grant all had malaria.

In Laura Ingalls Wilder's popular children's book *Little House on the Prairie* (based on Wilder's childhood in Kansas in the 1870s), Pa, Ma, Laura, and sister Mary all came down with fever and ague at the same time. Only a chance visit by a neighbor, who called in a doctor, saved their lives. The doctor apparently gave the family quinine, because Ingalls wrote that the medication she received was dreadfully bitter.

Historians believe that malaria peaked in the United States about 1875. But they estimate that in 1914, at least six hundred thousand cases still occurred each year.

Encouraged by the great success of the mosquito control program in Panama, U.S. public health officials began similar projects in the United States. In the 1930s, the U.S. government began a project called the Tennessee Valley Authority (TVA). The project involved building a series of dams and hydroelectric power plants in the Tennessee River valley. With its warm, wet climate, the region was a hotbed of malaria. The TVA used many of the mosquito-control measures practiced in Panama. By the end of the project, in 1947, malaria had almost vanished from the Tennessee Valley.

In 1947 the U.S. government began the National Malaria Eradication Program. By then only about fifteen thousand cases of malaria struck Americans each year. As part of the eradication program, workers sprayed a new insecticide, dichlorodiphenyltrichloroethane (DDT), in and around more than 4.5 million U.S. homes. DDT proved to be highly effective in killing mosquitoes.

Around this time, scientists developed chloroquine, a synthetic (human-made) version of quinine. Chloroquine quickly came into wide use in the United States. It proved very effective at preventing malaria and at treating the few people who still came down with the disease. In addition, Americans continued to drain wetlands and put screens on windows and doors. In 1950 U.S. health officials counted only about two thousand cases of malaria. In 1951 officials declared that malaria was gone from the United States.

Tackling Malaria Worldwide

Other wealthy nations, such as the countries of Western Europe, used similar programs to eradicate malaria. However, malaria was still a major problem in many poor nations, which did not have the resources to enact antimalaria programs.

In 1955 WHO launched the Global Malaria Eradication Program, a massive worldwide campaign. Its goal was to eliminate malaria within ten years. The program spent more than $1 billion on DDT and chloroquine. WHO workers sprayed thousands of tons of DDT around the world and gave chloroquine to many people who needed it.

The malaria eradication plan—one of the largest public health programs ever undertaken—met with spectacular success. The program conquered malaria in some places and sharply curbed it in others. It appeared—for a time—that people had won the battle against malaria.

Air pollution has caused global warming on Earth. As the planet gets warmer, malaria-carrying mosquitoes will move to newly warm areas.

Chapter 2

REEMERGING— WHY NOW?

The worldwide victory against malaria was short-lived. In the late twentieth century, the disease came storming back in many places on Earth. In parts of Africa, malaria increased by 40 percent between 1970 and 1997. The disease became more dangerous as well. It made people sicker than ever before.

Doctors call malaria a reemerging disease because it has returned to parts of the world where it once was well controlled. "Malaria was neglected for several decades," says Anthony Fauci, director of the U.S. National Institute of Allergy and Infectious Diseases, "but is now among the most important reemerging diseases worldwide."

What's responsible for the reemergence of malaria as a serious global threat to health and life? The better question is: who is responsible? And the answer is us. Human activities are among the main causes of malaria's reemergence. Experts say that future attempts to control or eradicate malaria cannot deal only with the disease itself. People must address the human factors as well.

Climate Change

Scientists believe that human activities—especially the burning of fossil fuels (coal, oil, and natural gas)—are leading to global warming. People burn fossil fuels to run vehicles and factories, to heat and cool buildings, and to cook food. People must find alternatives to fossil fuels, many believe. Otherwise, global temperatures could increase by 2 to 11°F (1 to 6°C) by the year 2100.

Mosquitoes thrive in warm weather, so higher temperatures would likely lead to larger mosquito populations. Studies suggest that temperature increases from 0.5 to 3°F (0.3 to 1.6°C) would double Earth's population of malaria-carrying mosquitoes. Warmer weather would also allow mosquitoes to extend their range. They could move into hills and mountains that were once too cool for them. More warm weather also gives mosquitoes a longer breeding season.

Scientists are seeing the effects of climate change all over the world. In the Andes Mountains of South America, "the pace of change is incredible," says Walter Vergara, climatologist (weather scientist) for the World Bank, an international lending organization. He notes that temperatures are increasing significantly faster at high altitudes than in the lowlands, setting the stage for malaria where it never before occurred.

"I'm talking about diseases at higher altitudes because the minimum night temperature is increasing," says Vergara. "In Colombia we have evidence that the malaria mosquito now is able to survive the night at 2,000 meters [6,600 feet]. This is one of the very sad stories of climate change in the mountains of the Andes. Those populations are going to be exposed to tropical diseases for the first time."[6]

Land Use

The global human population has grown from about 1.1 billion in 1850 to 6.75 billion in the early twenty-first century. As the population has increased, people have cut down forests to build homes, farms, and businesses. When people cut down forests, the animals living there leave or die. Some malaria-carrying mosquitoes prefer to feed on animal blood. But when animals are no longer available, mosquitoes turn to human blood instead.

This has happened along the Amazon River in Brazil. Since the late twentieth century, people have cut down millions of acres of rain forest near the river for farming, logging, and mining. As people have moved in, animals have disappeared from their rain forest homes. Mosquitoes have increasingly started to feed on humans instead of animals. So they have passed on malaria to more and more people. In

Over time, people have cleared jungles to create farms, homes, and businesses in places like the basin of the Amazon River in northern Peru (above). As people move into wilderness areas, mosquitoes feed on the newcomers and spread malaria.

addition, new dams and irrigation channels for watering crops provide additional places for mosquitoes to breed. In 1970 about fifty thousand people got malaria in Brazil. By 2006 that number had soared to more than one million each year.

People on the Move

Around the world, millions of people are constantly on the move because of war, famine, drought, and poverty. Worldwide, up to fifty million people may be refugees at any one time. They move from country to country or village to village in search of safety, food, and water. This constant flow of humanity carries malaria and other diseases along with it. Sometimes, infected people carry malaria into regions where the local residents have little immunity (natural resistance) to it. Conversely, people with little immunity to malaria sometimes move to areas where malaria is common. In one instance, health officials in Sudan reported 8,041 new cases of malaria in just one week. Most of the infected people lived in crowded refugee camps.

The increased speed and frequency of world travel also helps malaria spread. In earlier centuries, it took people months to circle the globe. They had to travel by sailing ship. Since people traveled slowly, diseases also traveled more slowly in those days.

In modern times, about eighteen million commercial airplane flights take off each year. They carry more than two billion people. Air passengers cross continents and oceans in just hours, sometimes carrying the malaria parasite within their blood. Millions more people travel by boat, train, private plane, and automobile. Malaria may ride along with them as well.

Tourists take a sightseeing trip to Bandhavgarh National Park in India. Traveling to countries where malaria is common can mean bringing it home with you.

Warfare

Warfare has also contributed to the reemergence of malaria around the world. The central Asian nation of Afghanistan, for instance, had nearly wiped out malaria by 1970. But when the former Soviet Union (fifteen republics that included Russia) invaded Afghanistan in 1979, antimalaria programs crumbled under the pressure of war.

In the twenty-first century, a few African nations are in a state of constant warfare. In these places, doctors and other health workers can't safely carry out malaria treatment or prevention programs. Médecins Sans Frontières (MSF, or Doctors Without Borders) is an international organization that provides medical care in many poor nations, including Somalia in northeastern

Africa. In July 2009, MSF announced that it was closing its largest health center in Somalia because of violence. "Somalia is a very difficult place to provide humanitarian assistance as was underlined by the abduction of two MSF medical staff...in April 2009," the organization explained in a press release. "Following the abduction and other serious incidents over the past year, MSF can no longer safely provide quality medical care to the people living in Bakool [a region of Somalia]. In just 14 months, MSF was forced to close four projects due to increasing insecurity including abductions and fatal attacks on our staff in Somalia. Risks there have reached unacceptable levels."

Resistance

Resistance is another reason for malaria's reemergence around the world. Malaria has become increasingly resistant to—or able to withstand—the medications commonly used to treat it. And the *Anopheles* mosquitoes that carry the *Plasmodium* parasite are growing resistant to the insecticides used to kill them.

Resistance to malaria medications can develop in several ways. In some cases, people unknowingly take fake malaria medications or don't take enough medication. The medicines kill off only the weakest malaria parasites in their bodies. The stronger, more resistant parasites remain alive. These strong parasites live on to reproduce, passing their resistance to medication to the next generation of parasites. Parasites can also become resistant to medications through natural mutation. Mutation is a sudden and natural change in the genetic material of an organism.

Because of poor or incomplete reporting, health officials are not certain exactly how many people suffer or die from malaria each year. Many poor people don't have access to medical clinics. They never get professional care for malaria and are not counted in case totals. In the end, the actual number of malaria cases is probably much higher than reported. By some estimates, only one out of five malaria deaths is reported worldwide.

Just as parasites can develop resistance to medication, mosquitoes can develop resistance to insecticides. Sometimes insecticides kill off only the weakest mosquitoes. The mosquitoes that resist the insecticides are the ones that reproduce and pass their resistance on to their offspring. As time goes on, people need stronger and stronger insecticides—and more of them—to kill the mosquitoes that carry malaria.

As malaria has reemerged, health organizations have changed their goals for malaria. WHO and other groups have determined that wiping out malaria worldwide is probably unrealistic. New goals are to reduce the number of malaria cases, provide better treatment for people who get malaria, and reduce the number of malaria deaths around the world.

These houses in a lake village in the African nation of Benin have no screens to keep out mosquitoes.

Chapter 3

MALARIA AROUND THE WORLD

From A to Z—Afghanistan to Zimbabwe—malaria threatens the people of 109 out of about 190 countries on Earth. That's about 3.2 billion people. Nearly half of the world's children live in malaria-stricken countries.

Perhaps as many as five hundred million people come down with malaria every year—although due to underreporting, the number might be much higher. Some people have several attacks of malaria each year. In some countries, half of all doctor visits are for malaria and nearly half of all hospital admissions are for malaria.

For malaria to flourish, a place must have a warm, wet climate and *Anopheles* mosquitoes. These conditions exist mainly in tropical and subtropical regions. Tropical regions are those near the equator, the imaginary line that divides Earth into the Northern Hemisphere and the Southern Hemisphere. Subtropical regions are just north and south of the tropics. In many tropical and subtropical countries, temperatures stay above 60°F (16°C) for much of the year.

Mosquitoes that carry malaria need standing or slow-moving water in which to lay their eggs. Countries that have wiped out malaria, such as the United States, are those that have drained water sources where mosquitoes breed. People in these countries have also controlled adult mosquito populations with insecticides. Lastly, they have covered windows and doors with screens to keep out mosquitoes.

But huge swaths of the world are always infested with malaria-carrying mosquitoes. In many of these places, poverty, warfare, and government inefficiency keep people from taking the steps needed to control malaria.

Malaria in Africa

Africa suffers from malaria more than any other continent. About 86 percent of the world's malaria cases occur in Africa. More than nine out of ten malaria deaths occur there as well. Most malaria cases in Africa occur in the sub-Saharan region, the part of Africa lying south of the Sahara, the world's largest hot desert.

Large parts of sub-Saharan Africa have a warm, humid climate. They are perfect places for malaria-carrying mosquitoes. The deadliest form of malaria, spread by the

MALARIA IN SUB-SAHARAN AFRICA

Country	Population	Percent of People at Risk for Malaria	Number of Confirmed Cases per Year
Nigeria	141,000,000	100	57,506,000
Kenya	37,000,000	76	11,342,000
Mozambique	20,800,000	100	7,433,000
Ghana	23,500,000	100	7,282,000
Ivory Coast	20,000,000	100	7,029,000
Zambia	12,200,000	100	3,655,000

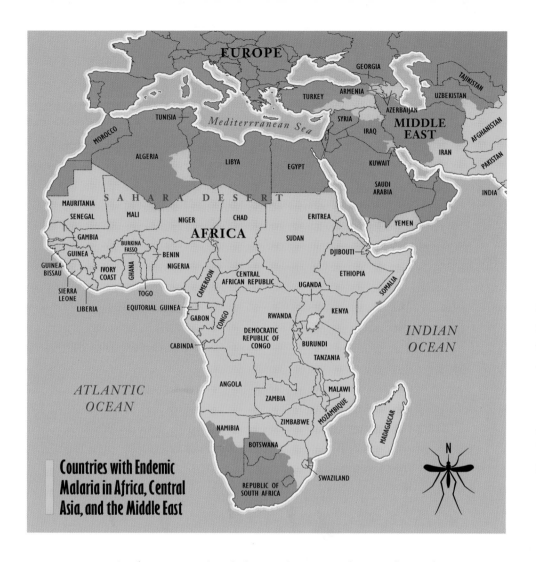

Countries with Endemic Malaria in Africa, Central Asia, and the Middle East

mosquito known as *Anopheles gambiae*, is widespread in sub-Saharan Africa. In most of sub-Saharan Africa, malaria has become resistant to many common malaria medications. These factors make malaria, rather than HIV/AIDs, the primary health concern in much of sub-Saharan Africa.

Depending on the location, the malaria season in sub-Saharan Africa—the time during which mosquitoes spread malaria—can range from two to twelve months of the year.

Life expectancy in many parts of Africa is extremely low. In Zambia, for instance, people can expect to live only about thirty-nine years. In Mozambique life expectancy is about forty-one years. Compare these numbers to the United States, where life expectancy is about seventy-eight years. Malaria is just one reason for the low life expectancy of many Africans. HIV/AIDS, tuberculosis, and other infectious diseases, as well as poverty, lack of health care, and malnutrition, are also to blame.

"During every rainy season, the children in my village would drop like flies, struck down by malaria," says the religious leader of a village in southern Mali. "I had to bury them two at a time, there were so many deaths."

Northern Africa includes the nations of Morocco, Algeria, Tunisia, Libya, and Egypt. The vast Sahara covers much of these nations. The dry desert climate makes them inhospitable for mosquitoes. Malaria is largely under control in this area.

IRAN

Malaria in Southern Asia

While the majority of malaria cases occur in sub-Saharan Africa, about two-thirds of the rest occur in southern Asia, in places such as Bangladesh, India, Indonesia, Myanmar (Burma), and Thailand. "Malaria is the disease of the poor, and half of the developing world's poor live in [southern] Asia," says former WHO regional director Samlee Plianbangchang. "Together, Bangladesh and eastern India have as many poor people as all of sub-Saharan Africa."

More than four million cases of malaria occur in southern

Asia each year. Most occur in India, Indonesia, and Myanmar. India reported more than one million cases of malaria in 2008.

Southeast Asia has fewer malaria deaths than Africa, because the region has a less dangerous type of malaria parasite. On the negative side, Southeast Asia has the highest rates of drug and insecticide resistance in the world. "If we do not put a stop to the drug-resistant malaria situation that has been documented along the Thai-Cambodian border, it could spread rapidly to our neighboring countries and threaten our efforts to control this deadly disease," writes Hiroki Nakatani of the World Health Organization.

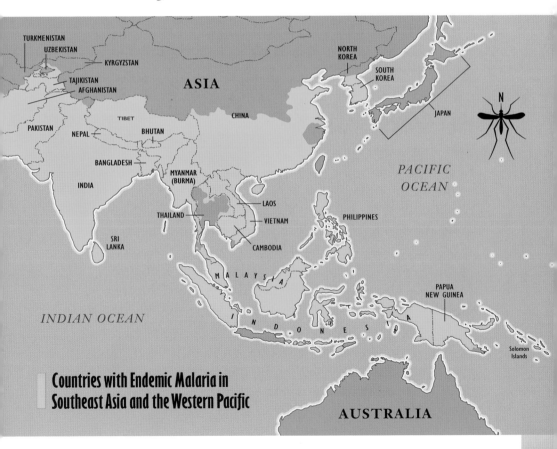

Countries with Endemic Malaria in Southeast Asia and the Western Pacific

Malaria in Central Asia

Malaria is a significant problem in the nations of central Asia. In Afghanistan, where malaria was once under control, the disease has reemerged. It is common in Afghan river valleys, where farmers grow rice in irrigated fields. In this nation of thirty-two million people, more than 600,000 cases of malaria occurred in Afghanistan in 2002. By 2007, due to better malaria control programs, that number had declined to 430,000 cases. But the country needs to make much more progress.

Malaria is also a major problem in Pakistan. The nation had at least 125,000 malaria cases per year in the early 2000s. Health officials are also concerned about malaria in Turkey, Tajikistan, Azerbaijan, and Georgia. These central Asian nations have not yet wiped out malaria, but the number of cases seems to be declining.

Malaria in Eastern Asia and the Pacific

The eastern Asia/Pacific region includes southern China, Cambodia, Vietnam, Papua New Guinea, the Philippines, and other countries. Either in full or in part, these countries have the wet, warm weather that malaria-carrying mosquitoes prefer. In China about half the population is at risk for malaria. The risk climbs to nearly 100 percent in Papua New Guinea and the Solomon Islands. Although Australia is also part of this region, experts consider it free of malaria.

The region had an estimated 1.75 million cases of malaria in 2008. Most of them occurred in Cambodia, China, Papua New Guinea, the Solomon Islands, and Vietnam. Yet death from malaria in this region is quite low compared to

Africa. Medical care tends to be better in the eastern Asia/
Pacific region than in Africa and southern Asia. The form of
malaria that circulates in this region is also less dangerous
than malaria in other regions.

Malaria in Europe

Experts consider Western Europe to be free of malaria,
but sometimes refugees and international travelers arrive
there with malaria. In the twenty-first century, ten
thousand to twelve thousand cases of such "imported
malaria" occur in Western Europe each year. Many places
in northern and Eastern Europe are too cold for the
mosquitoes that spread malaria.

Malaria in the Americas

Malaria is present in nearly every country south of the
United States, from Mexico through Central and South
America. This region also includes the islands of the
Caribbean Sea.

According to the Pan American Health Organization
(the WHO branch in the Americas), South America had
approximately 572,000 cases of malaria in 2008. Making
the situation worse, 80 percent of malaria cases in South
America are resistant to the most common malaria
medications. Brazil has by far the most serious malaria
problem in the Americas. More than half the region's
malaria cases occur in Brazil.

Among the Caribbean islands, malaria is always present
in Haiti and the Dominican Republic, which together make
up the island of Hispaniola. Occasionally, outbreaks occur

Countries with Endemic Malaria in the Americas

on other islands as well. Outbreaks occurred in the Bahamas and Jamaica in 2006 and 2007.

Most of Canada and some parts of the United States are too cold for the mosquitoes that transmit malaria. However, the types of *Anopheles* mosquitoes that spread malaria in the past are still common in many warm, southern states. The reemergence of malaria in warmer states is a very real possibility.

Between 2002 and 2007, U.S. public health officials reported an average of 1,423 cases of malaria each year. Most of the cases were imported malaria, which Americans caught when traveling to malarial countries. The travelers returned home and fell sick a few days or weeks later. In a few cases, local mosquitoes have bitten people with imported malaria, picked up the malaria parasite, and gone on to infect other people.

In cases of so-called airport malaria, infected mosquitoes enter countries hidden in cargo holds of planes and boats. The infected mosquitoes bite healthy people who live around harbors and airports. In the United States, most reported cases of airport malaria have occurred in California, New York, New Jersey, and Florida—all states with major seaports and major international airports.

A mother and baby lie under a mosquito net in the African country of Guinea.

Chapter 4

A DISEASE OF POVERTY

Malaria can sicken and kill anyone—from newborns to the elderly. People of both genders and all races have equal risk of getting malaria. But people living in poverty are more likely to get malaria than are people who are better off. Poor families often cannot afford to put screens on their windows and doorways to keep out mosquitoes. Many cannot afford bed nets (netting to drape over their beds) to keep mosquitoes from biting them at night. People in poor, malaria-stricken areas often lack transportation to get to health clinics—or have no nearby health clinics. All too often, poor people cannot afford the medications needed to prevent and treat malaria. "Malaria is a terrible tragedy that is visited repeatedly on the poor of the world," says Dr. Terrence Smith. "All of us are very frustrated that after all this time, there isn't better control of malaria so as to prevent depriving so many children of a healthy future."

Malaria is both a disease of poverty and a cause of poverty. It makes poor people even poorer. A person who is sick with malaria cannot go to work, tend crops, or care for animals. Parents who are sick with malaria can't care for their children. Children sick with malaria cannot attend school regularly.

A young boy with malaria gets treatment at a hospital in Colombia, South America.

They cannot gain enough education to rise out of a cycle of poverty and illness as adults. If a parent dies of malaria, his or her children are more likely to grow up in poverty.

In malaria-stricken areas, governments and aid organizations spend money on mosquito-control activities, malaria prevention, and research into the disease. Often governments fund health clinics and distribute bed nets and medications to their poor citizens. Countries with the most malaria spend up to 40 percent of their public health money on the disease. But these efforts often fall short. Because of poor transportation systems, government inefficiency, poor public health systems, and warfare, supplies and medications don't always reach the people who need them.

In some places, communities can't afford even the most basic malaria-prevention measures. The small Nigerian town of Hadejia, for instance, has a subpar drainage system. "The few drains in town are full," says one resident, leaving standing water where mosquitoes breed. He continues,

"People are dying from malaria due to the stagnant water in every nook and cranny of the town."

In addition to sickening and killing people, malaria impacts countries in other ways. Tourists may avoid visiting a malarious region for fear of getting the disease. Wealthy foreign investors may not want to open factories or start other businesses in areas with a lot of malaria. Investors know that workers will often be out ill with malaria—and that is bad for

MALARIA AND HIV INFECTION

Malaria and HIV/AIDS are perhaps the most challenging global health problems of our time. Combined, these diseases kill about four million people each year. The malaria parasite and HIV (human immunodeficiency virus, which causes AIDS) are widespread in the same regions: sub-Saharan Africa, Southeast Asia, Latin America, and the Caribbean. In these regions, it is common for a person to have both infections.

Because HIV weakens the immune system, people who have both HIV and malaria are much sicker than those who have only one of the diseases. HIV infection also reduces the effectiveness of malaria medications and allows the number of malaria parasites to increase. Similarly, malaria infection worsens HIV infection by increasing the viral load—the amount of HIV in the body.

Health officials say that HIV and malaria programs should cooperate closely to identify people with dual (double) infection. When people with one disease seek medical care, they should be tested for the other disease. This testing helps ensure that people get early diagnosis and treatment. People with dual infection also need treatment by specialists, who know how to prevent harmful reactions between malaria and HIV drugs.

business. Jarbas Barbosa, who works for the Pan American Health Organization, sums up the situation this way, "Malaria is a problem not only for health, but also for social and economic development."

How and Who

Most people get malaria from the bite of infected mosquitoes. But mosquito bites are not the only way to get malaria. The parasite can pass from an infected person to a healthy one through dirty hypodermic needles. This kind of infection can happen when people share needles to inject drugs or when health-care workers reuse needles and syringes without sterilizing them. Some health clinics in poor countries cannot afford to buy new needles and syringes for each person and may use one needle several times. On rare occasions, people get malaria from transplanted organs or from donated blood.

In addition to these routes of transmission, mothers can pass malaria to their babies before or during birth. Where malaria is very common, many babies are born with malaria parasites in their blood. Children who are not born with malaria are susceptible to it. In some African nations, seven out of ten babies have malaria parasites in their blood by their first birthday. The vast majority of malaria deaths and severe illnesses occur in sub-Saharan African children under the age of five.

Leo Ho, an MSF pediatrician, worked at a hospital in the Bo region of Sierra Leone, a nation in western Africa and one of the poorest countries in the world. He describes the tragic toll that malaria takes on children in particular. "Quite frequently, little children would come in comatose,

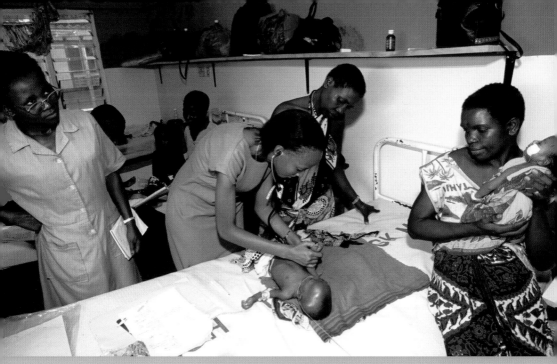

A doctor at a clinic in Kenya examines a baby with malaria and pneumonia, while the baby's mother *(back right)* watches. Another mother and child sick with malaria *(front right)* watch and wait.

just incredibly sick," he says. "Sometimes, the infection is so severe, it can progress over a day or over a few hours where a child can be sitting up, alert, and then, hours later, in a coma. Or, a lot of parents wait before they bring their children in. Often, they wait until the child became non-responsive before coming to the hospital. We saw a lot of this and it's just really unfortunate because, obviously, the later they came in, the less we could do."

Ho continues. "We would have at least two children die at our hospital every day on average, sometimes more. And it would happen so unexpectedly. When a child died, he or she would be wrapped up in a lappa, the same cloth that held them against their mothers' backs when they were well. But many of our patients got better, also."

In some African countries, more than one-third of all young children are sick with malaria at any one time. For children without proper treatment, malaria usually comes and goes in regular cycles, making them sick three, four, five, or more times each year. These periods of illness force children to miss school. They fall behind in their studies. They miss out on other daily activities, such as playtime and family time.

At its worst, malaria can leave children with permanent brain damage, seizures, blindness, stunted growth, paralysis

SUCCESS STORIES

Malawi is a nation in East Africa. In some places, 50 to 70 percent of Malawian children suffer from malaria at any one time. To combat the disease, the international aid organization Save the Children has provided malaria treatment kits to thirty-three schools in Malawi's Mangochi District. Aid workers have trained teachers to diagnose the disease and give pills to sick children. Children know they can go to school and get treatment as soon as they begin to feel ill.

The people of Mangochi say this program has been good for children, families, and the community. "I like the kit at school because after treatment I become happy again, get better and go back to school, play and I can do my work," said one thirteen-year-old girl. Parents like the school-based program because it saves them a difficult trip on foot to the nearest health center, which for some is a daylong journey. Children who are healthy can also help their families with chores such as feeding animals, carrying water, and caring for younger siblings.

Community leaders say that school enrollments are up

of one or both arms or legs, or severe anemia (a shortage of oxygen-carrying red blood cells). Once malaria weakens the body, other diseases are likely to follow. Some experts believe that nearly every child in sub-Saharan Africa is in some way physically or mentally damaged by malaria. This damage to children hurts African societies as a whole.

Pregnant women are susceptible to severe malaria because pregnancy weakens the body's immune system—the system that fights off disease. And malaria may sicken not only the pregnant woman but also her fetus (the developing baby).

and absenteeism is down. "The change I see is that now more parents are sending their children to the school because they know the children will get treated without delay when they are sick," says Mai Hawa, a village leader. "This is a good thing for our community. I will continue to support the kits."

In rural villages of the Philippines, another program is making a big difference. There, the Global Fund to Fight AIDS, Tuberculosis and Malaria has trained about three hundred women as microscopists. They use microscopes to detect the malaria parasite in blood samples. Most of these women have little or no formal education but have become skilled at their jobs. "These women are given five weeks of training on the basics of how to do a blood smear [a test for malaria], how to read the results, and how to take care of the microscope," says program manager Marvi Trudeau. "After the training, they take the microscope back to their villages. When people have malaria symptoms, they go to the . . . microscopist. Within 30 minutes, they are given the results of the test, and receive the medication they need for free." This program is drastically reducing malaria cases and malaria deaths in the region.

When malaria parasites infect red blood cells, the cells become damaged and misshapen. In a pregnant woman, the damaged red blood cells can clog the placenta and the umbilical cord, which supply the fetus with oxygen and food. If the placenta and umbilical cord are damaged, the fetus cannot grow and develop normally.

If the mother has anemia, the fetus might not get enough oxygen. It might not grow to a healthy size. Malaria in pregnancy can also lead to miscarriage, prematurity, low birth weight, or stillbirth (delivery of a fully formed but dead infant). "Malaria remains one of the most important threats to the health of pregnant women and their newborns," concludes Carol Bellamy, former executive director of the United Nations Children's Fund, also known as UNICEF.

Once and Again

Some diseases affect people only once. For instance, after a person gets measles, he or she will not get it again. Malaria works differently. If you get bitten by an infected mosquito, you will get malaria, even if you've had the disease before.

People who live in areas where malaria is endemic, or constantly present, will be infected repeatedly during their lifetimes. Each time they are infected, their bodies will build up a little more immunity to future infections. As immunity develops over the years, malaria symptoms become less severe. A baby who gets malaria for the first time will be much sicker than an adult who gets it for the tenth time or the twentieth. In countries with endemic malaria, once children reach ten years old, they usually have enough immunity to keep them from ever becoming severely ill with malaria.

A young girl cries as her finger is pricked during a malaria test in Myanmar in 2009.

Most women who live in areas of endemic malaria get malaria several times in childhood. They reach their childbearing years with some immunity to malaria. These women are less likely to become ill or die from malaria during pregnancy. With each additional pregnancy, they build up more immunity to the disease. However, women living in areas of epidemic malaria—where malaria strikes less often but affects many people when it does strike—have much less immunity. If these women have never had malaria before, they may become very ill or even die from malaria during pregnancy.

The Cycle of Poverty

In much of the world, people live in extreme poverty. Nurse Mary McMahon, founder of the humanitarian group Nurses for the Nations, has worked in some of the world's poorest villages. She describes a scene along the Amazon River in Brazil:

> The villagers suffer from extreme poverty and life threatening illnesses. In the jungle, life expectancy is 45 years. People are sick with malaria, dengue fever, hepatitis, and worm infestations. Simple huts are built with wood planks and grass roofs. As many as 8–10 family members can live in one house. There is no furniture, stove, sink, bathtub, or beds. The people sleep on handmade hammocks, sometimes criss-crossed one on top of each other. People must use the Amazon River and the jungle floor as their toilets. They also use the river for drinking, bathing, washing clothes, and fishing. Hand-made wooden boats are the only source of transportation. Most of the Amazon people have no shoes and very little clothing.

If they are sick with malaria and other diseases, children cannot thrive. They cannot concentrate in school. They cannot focus on learning job skills. Even if they manage to survive malaria and other diseases in childhood, they are likely to remain in poverty as adults.

People in poor nations often face an uphill battle in fighting malaria. Josué is a seventeen-year-old in the western African nation of Togo. He learned about malaria in school. He knows that mosquitoes spread malaria and that the disease can be prevented. However, many people in this village don't have this basic information, and the information they do have is based on rumor and superstition. In Josué's village, some elders even tell people that "mothers use too much red oil [palm oil] in their sauces, that's why babies have malaria."

Josué laments that "each year, children die and are buried. However, malaria is an illness that people can avoid and fight." He wants to teach his fellow villagers the facts about malaria. "It's our duty to fight for the life of children and adults," he says.

Young people like Josué will be critical in the future fight against malaria. Better education about the disease will lead to fewer malaria cases and fewer deaths. Less malaria will mean fewer sick children, more children who succeed in school, and fewer people living in poverty. When people rise out of poverty, they are more likely to be able to afford and to take the measures needed to prevent and treat malaria. In this way, the cycle of malaria and poverty can be broken.

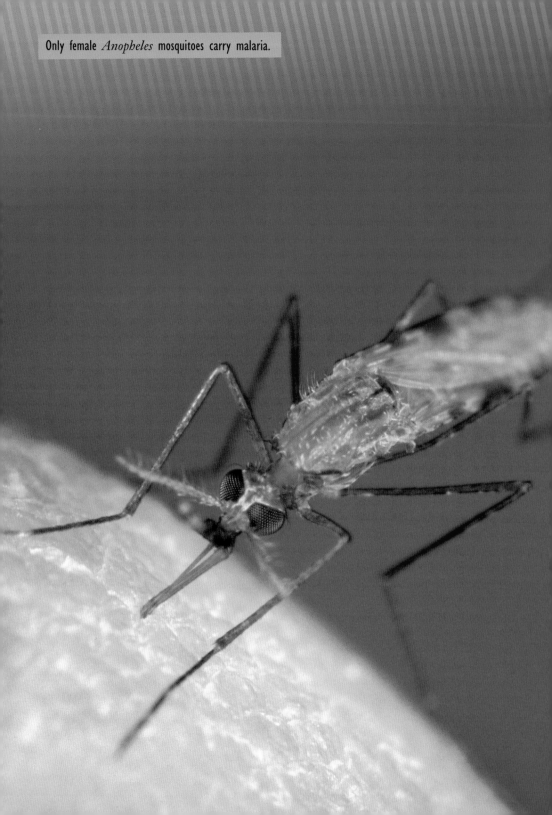

Only female *Anopheles* mosquitoes carry malaria.

Chapter 5

A MOSQUITO MEAL

People are nothing more than a meal for the *Anopheles* mosquito and the malaria parasite it carries. The relationship among humans, mosquitoes, and malaria parasites is so complex that it escaped detection for centuries. Even in the twenty-first century, we have a lot to learn. One day we will probably control malaria through a combination of effective vaccines, better medications, and improved insecticides. Until then the more we know about the lethal cycle of the malaria–human relationship, the more lives we can save.

The Mosquitoes

Mosquitoes are members of a group of animals called arthropods. They are related to lobsters, spiders, and fleas. About thirty-five hundred species of mosquitoes inhabit Earth. More than four hundred of those species are *Anopheles* mosquitoes, but only thirty to forty of the *Anopheles* species carry malaria.

In addition, only female *Anopheles* mosquitoes transmit malaria. Male *Anopheles* mosquitoes are harmless. They feed on nectar and other sources of sugar with their simple mouthparts. Females are the dangerous ones. Nectar is their second food choice. What they really need is blood. Female mosquitoes have long, intricate mouthparts adapted for piercing the skin of their victims and drinking their blood. In the process of feeding, female *Anopheles* can transmit not only malaria but also other dangerous diseases such as yellow fever, dengue fever, West Nile virus, and several forms of encephalitis.

Like all mosquitoes, the *Anopheles* has a four-stage life cycle: egg, larva, pupa, and adult. The first three stages require water. Mosquitoes can fly only 2 miles (3 km) at most, so after mating, a female mosquito must find nearby water in which to lay her eggs. The water can be a quiet pond or a marsh, a flooded rice field, an irrigation ditch, or even rainwater collected in an old tire in someone's yard. The mosquito requires only that the water be fairly still. The mosquito lays fifty to two hundred eggs at a time. She deposits them on the water's surface, where they float until hatching.

A mosquito control analyst in Florida points out the tiny brown larvae of the *Anopheles* mosquito in water from a drainage ditch. Two men who lived near the area got sick with malaria.

Hatching takes two to three days in hot weather and two to three weeks in cooler weather. In colder climates, the eggs can lie dormant (inactive) in winter and not hatch until spring. The eggs hatch into larvae, which are legless, wingless, and wormlike. Each larva has a head with mouth brushes, which it uses to eat algae, bacteria, and other creatures smaller than itself. The larvae float belly up on the water's surface, breathing through tiny holes in their abdomens. Larger insects and fish eat most of the larvae.

A few days after hatching, the surviving larvae turn into comma-shaped pupae. Each pupa has an abdomen, and a head and thorax (chest) merged into a structure called a cephalothorax. In another few days, the cephalothorax splits open and the adult mosquito emerges. The adult has the three distinct parts of an insect: head, thorax, and abdomen, plus six legs and wings. After becoming an adult, the mosquito leaves the water and flies to a nearby tree or bush to rest.

Mosquitoes can develop from egg to adult in as little as five days. On average, the process takes ten to fourteen days. Mosquitoes begin mating two or three days into adulthood. The males form large swarms at dusk, and the females fly into the swarms to mate. Females need to mate only once to produce eggs for the rest of their lives.

After mating, the females begin searching for food. Like males, female *Anopheles* mosquitoes eat nectar for energy. But they also need the protein found in blood for their developing eggs. Some mosquitoes feed only on the blood of birds and other animals. For other mosquitoes—the ones that transmit human malaria—people top the menu.

Mosquitoes don't see very well, but they don't need to. The carbon dioxide (CO_2) and moisture that humans exhale attract mosquitoes. Mosquitoes can sense CO_2 from

Born in France, Nathalie Mvondo spent most of her childhood in the African nation of Cameroon. She recalls getting malaria a lot. "I had malaria once or twice a year when I lived in Cameroon, always during the summer rainy season when the mosquitoes were on parade. I tried to cover up and to watch out for them, but I was just a kid. We lived in the country part of the time, where we had to go to the river to get our water. It was a lot of fun, but it came with a price—mosquito bites all over my legs. Those mosquitoes loved to feed on me!"

Nathalie's parents gave her the medication chloroquine to keep her from getting malaria, but it didn't always work. The malaria parasite in Cameroon is resistant to chloroquine. And you can give a little kid only so much medicine. "When I came down with malaria I got extremely weak and had really bad muscle aches," Nathalie says. "I'd get a high fever and would shiver from the cold, even though the weather was very hot. Sometimes I would lose consciousness."

Nathalie remembers being in the hospital a few times. "The pills were too big for my mouth, and they were very, very bitter. Sometimes they gave me syrup that was even worse. The nurses dripped fluids into my veins and that helped me get better a lot faster. I was really into sports, strong and full of life when I was a child, and the malaria kept me from doing what I wanted to do when I was sick. It always seemed like an eternity before I got well."

about 100 feet (30 m) away. They're also attracted to the smell of certain chemicals in our sweat and to the warmth coming from our bodies. Using sensors on their antennae, mosquitoes can detect our body heat.

Let's say a female mosquito lands on a human foot kicked out from under the covers. She finds an area where the blood is close to the surface—perhaps the tender skin on the top of the foot. The mosquito pierces the skin with tiny tools on her proboscis, or feeding tube. She injects the skin with saliva mixed with an anticoagulant, a chemical to keep the blood from clotting. That chemical is what makes mosquito bites so itchy and irritating.

Next, the mosquito inserts her proboscis into a small blood vessel. She settles down to feed on the moving blood. It takes about ten minutes for the mosquito to eat her fill. And it takes a lot to fill her up. A mosquito takes in two to three times her body weight in blood with each feeding. That's like you chugging down a bathtub full of orange juice.

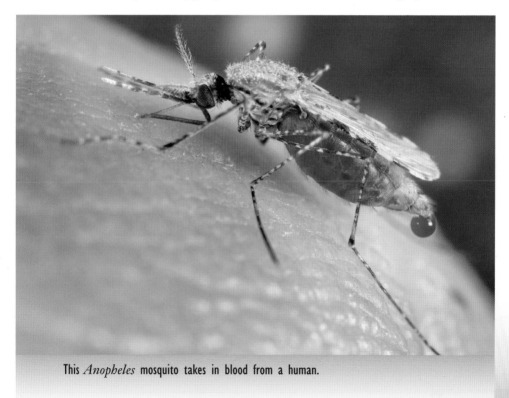

This *Anopheles* mosquito takes in blood from a human.

After feeding, the mosquito must rest while she digests the blood and her eggs develop. Many mosquitoes that feed on humans rest high on the walls inside houses. The eggs inside her body take about three days to develop. The mosquito then finds the necessary water, lays her eggs, and then begins seeking her next blood meal. If no one swats her, if another creature doesn't eat her, or if insecticides don't poison her, the mosquito repeats this process several times in her two- to four-week life.

The Parasites

Plasmodium, the parasite that causes malaria, is a one-celled organism. It has a complex life cycle that requires both mosquitoes and animals or humans. More than one hundred *Plasmodium* species live on Earth. They infect a wide variety of animals, but only four of them commonly infect humans.

Plasmodium falciparum (P. falciparum) lives worldwide in tropical and subtropical regions. All four types of human malaria parasites can be deadly, but *P. falciparum* is by far the most dangerous. It causes about half of all malaria cases and more than 90 percent of malaria deaths. The parasite reproduces rapidly and may cause serious anemia by wrecking red blood cells. The parasites can also clog small blood vessels in the brain, leading to deadly cerebral malaria.

Plasmodium vivax (P. vivax) is the most widespread of the *Plasmodium* parasites. It occurs in tropical, subtropical, and temperate (cooler) regions. It is the most common cause of malaria in the United States. *P. vivax* has a dormant stage in which the parasite enters the liver. During this stage, its growth and activity nearly stop. It can reactivate and leave the liver to cause malaria months or even years after the bite

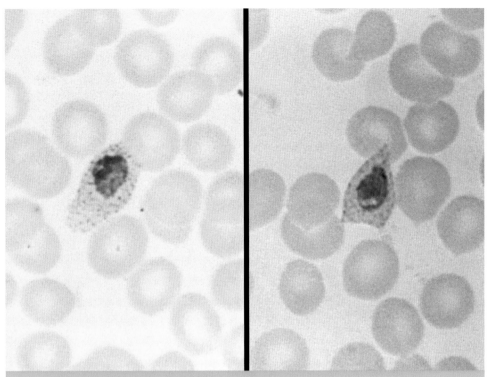

These images show *Plasmodium ovale*. This form of malaria turns round blood cells into ovals (dark cells in center of both images).

of an infected mosquito. People rarely die from *P. vivax*, but it often makes people sick on and off for years.

Plasmodium ovale (P. ovale) lives mostly in sub-Saharan Africa and islands of the western Pacific. It earned its name because it distorts normally round red blood cells into an oval shape. Like *P. vivax*, *P. ovale* can remain dormant in the liver for several months. Even without treatment, the immune system of a healthy person usually clears this parasite from the body in about one year.

Plasmodium malariae (P. malariae) occurs in the same locations as the other parasites. Left untreated, *P. malariae* seldom kills. Instead, it may sicken a person on and off for twenty years or even a lifetime.

International public health officials are worried about a new kind of malaria that apparently crossed over from monkeys to humans in the late 1990s. Called *Plasmodium knowlesi (P. knowlesi)*, this parasite normally infects long-tailed macaques, monkeys that live in Southeast Asian rain forests. It rivals deadly *P. falciparum* in its severity. The parasite reproduces every twenty-four hours and infects great numbers of red blood cells. In a study of one thousand people in Southeast Asia with malaria, about 25 percent were sick with this newly identified form of malaria. Some scientists are already calling *P. knowlesi* the fifth human malaria parasite.

The Cycle of Infection

If a mosquito other than an *Anopheles* bites a person with malaria, the mosquito digests the malaria parasites, thus killing them. But if an *Anopheles* mosquito bites a person with malaria, the mosquito cannot digest the parasites. They remain alive within the mosquito's body. That's why *Plasmodium* is successful in *Anopheles* mosquitoes but not in other species. The parasites may weaken the infected mosquito or shorten its life. But as long as it is alive, the infected *Anopheles* mosquito will spread the parasites to a new host with each bite.

As the parasite moves between mosquito and human, it goes through several stages of development within each host. From human to mosquito to human and back again, there is no clear beginning or end to the cycle of infection. So let's start with that itchy mosquito bite that's heralded by an annoying high-pitched whine.

Like a mosquito, which takes several different forms

during its lifetime, *Plasmodium* parasites go through several different stages. Inside an infected mosquito's saliva, the parasite is in the sporozoite stage. Sporozoites are so tiny that fifty thousand of them could fit into the period at the end of this sentence. The infected mosquito's salivary gland is jam-packed with one hundred thousand *Plasmodium* sporozoites. Each time the mosquito injects her saliva into a human host, a few dozen sporozoites enter as well. It takes only one sporozoite to cause malaria.

Within the first thirty to sixty minutes after a bite, the sporozoites travel through the infected person's bloodstream to the liver. Each sporozoite enters a liver cell and changes into a schizont. The schizont devours the contents of the liver cell. In about a week, the mature schizont divides into a dozen or more merozoites. The merozoite is the next stage of the parasite's life cycle.

The merozoites burst from the ruined liver cell and rush into the bloodstream. This is when malaria victims suffer from fever and chills for the first time. If the parasite is *P. vivax* or *P. ovale*, hypnozoites (another stage) can remain dormant in the liver. Hypnozoites can emerge from the liver months or years later to cause malaria.

After leaving the liver, the merozoites quickly find and enter red blood cells. The human immune system does not attack its own red blood cells, so the merozoites are safe once they are inside. Within the red blood cells, merozoites change into trophozoites. They feed on oxygen-carrying hemoglobin—the substance that gives red blood cells their color. After one to four days (depending on the *Plasmodium* species), the trophozoites morph into merozoites.

The Life Cycle of *Plasmodium*

Plasmodium (the malaria parasite) passes through several different stages within its hosts.

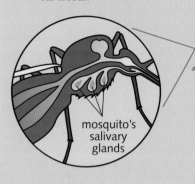

mosquito's salivary glands

1. Microscopic, threadlike *Plasmodium* sporozoites swim in a mosquito's saliva. They enter the bloodstream of a human when the insect bites. The sporozoites travel through the blood to the liver, where each one enters a liver cell.

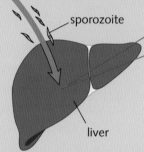

sporozoite

liver

MOSQUITO STAGE

sporozoite

ruined oocyst

9. The gametes then join together. Each fertilized oocyst divides into thousands of new sporozoites, which can then infect the next host that the mosquito bites.

fertilized zygote

8. A mosquito drinks in gametocytes when it bites the host. In the mosquito's stomach, the gametocytes produce gametes—male and female reproductive cells.

female gamete

male gamete

skin of host

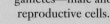

gametocytes

7. After several generations, the parasites begin sexual reproduction. Some merozoites transform themselves into gametocytes, cells that can produce reproductive cells.

2. Inside the liver cell, the sporozoite changes into a schizont. It devours the cell's contents.

3. After about one week, the mature schizont divides into a dozen or more merozoites—another infective stage. The merozoites break out of the liver cell and enter the blood-stream, causing a malaria attack.

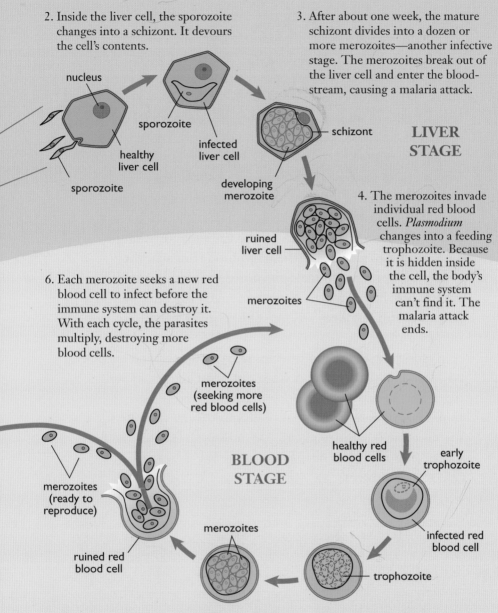

nucleus

sporozoite

healthy liver cell

infected liver cell

sporozoite

developing merozoite

schizont

LIVER STAGE

ruined liver cell

4. The merozoites invade individual red blood cells. *Plasmodium* changes into a feeding trophozoite. Because it is hidden inside the cell, the body's immune system can't find it. The malaria attack ends.

merozoites

6. Each merozoite seeks a new red blood cell to infect before the immune system can destroy it. With each cycle, the parasites multiply, destroying more blood cells.

merozoites (seeking more red blood cells)

BLOOD STAGE

healthy red blood cells

early trophozoite

merozoites (ready to reproduce)

ruined red blood cell

merozoites

infected red blood cell

trophozoite

5. After one to four days—depending on the species—the trophozoite divides to form merozoites. The ruined red blood cell bursts open, spilling the merozoites and their wastes into the bloodstream. Perhaps because merozoites mature at a similar rate, they all break out of the blood cells at about the same time. The synchronized timing gives malaria its characteristic symptoms—bouts of chills and fever alternating with periods when the victim feels better.

The merozoites destroy and burst from the red blood cells and then search for fresh ones. This process may go on for days, as merozoites seek new red blood cells and burst out of them. This constant destruction of red blood cells often results in severe anemia. The body cannot make new red blood cells fast enough to keep up with the destruction caused by malaria parasites. Every time merozoites enter the bloodstream, another bout of fever and chills begins.

After several cycles, some of the merozoites turn into cells called gametocytes. When a female mosquito bites an infected person, she sucks up the gametocytes along with human blood. Inside the mosquito's stomach, the gametocytes turn into male and female gametes. A male gamete fertilizes a female gamete in much the same way as a human sperm fertilizes an egg. The result is a fertilized egg called a zygote.

Zygotes dig deep into the mosquito's stomach and become oocysts. The sturdy oocyst stage can resist the mosquito's digestive juices. Soon the oocysts rupture and release thousands of new sporozoites. The sporozoites migrate to the mosquito's salivary gland. The mosquito spreads the sporozoites when she bites her next victim. The cycle of infection continues.

IMMUNITY AND VACCINES

The human immune system protects our bodies from the millions of dangerous organisms that attack us every day. Several types of white blood cells make up the first line of defense. These vital cells circulate in the bloodstream along with red blood cells.

An immune reaction begins when organisms called microbes enter the body through a break in the skin. The invaders can also enter in food or water or in the air we breathe. Our white blood cells chase down the invaders and destroy many of them.

Suppose the measles virus enters a little girl's body. White blood cells in her immune system help fight and kill much of the virus. She will get sick from the measles, but if she has a healthy immune system, she will likely recover.

After the child gets measles, her body's second line of defense kicks into action. Her immune system makes antibodies, which are proteins that fight foreign invaders. If the measles virus attacks the girl again, her immune system will remember the virus and send out antimeasles antibodies to fight off the infection. The girl will not get sick this time because she has become immune to measles.

In some cases, we don't have to get sick from a disease to become immune to it. That's where vaccines come in. Vaccines are medications made from killed or weakened microbes. The measles vaccine, for instance, is made from a weakened form of the measles virus. Doctors or nurses usually administer vaccines with injections. Inside the body, vaccines stimulate the immune system to form antibodies against certain kinds of diseases.

Suppose that a little boy has never had measles. Instead, he receives the measles vaccine when he is very young. His body makes antibodies against measles. If he is exposed to measles in the future, he will not get sick. He is immune to measles.

A woman in Zimbabwe receives mosquito nets. The charity Oxfam International distributed the nets.

Chapter 6

PREVENTING MALARIA

Even though more people are getting malaria than ever before and more people are dying of it, malaria remains a largely preventable disease. Wiping out malaria is unlikely in the near future. But protective measures can help control the parasite and the mosquito that carries it.

Personal Protection

People can protect themselves from mosquito bites using low-tech measures. Just paying attention to the time of day can help. Mosquitoes prefer to feed at dawn and dusk, although some bite all night long. In malaria-stricken areas, it's safest to stay indoors when mosquitoes are most active.

Screens on doors and windows help keep out mosquitoes and other insects. But in many countries, doors and windows may lack screens and simply be open to the outdoors. Or they may be draped with fabric, allowing easy access for mosquitoes.

In mosquito-infested areas, clothing that covers arms and legs protects people against bites, although this clothing is not always comfortable in extremely hot climates. Dark colors attract mosquitoes, so people in mosquito-infested

A man in Louisiana rubs insect repellent on his arm. In many poor nations, people can't afford insect repellent.

areas should avoid them. People who have access to insect repellent should spray it on their clothing and skin. Some manufacturers even make clothing from insecticide-treated fabric. But people in malaria-stricken countries often don't have access to such clothes and can't afford them. They might not be able to afford insect repellent.

Perhaps the best mosquito-protection device is the bed net. People hang bed nets from ceilings or walls. They drape the nets around beds, cots, or sleeping mats and tuck them in at the bottom to keep mosquitoes out of sleeping spaces.

Health officials recommend that in malaria-stricken areas, every child under five years old and every pregnant woman sleep under a bed net. Nets treated with insecticides are twice as effective at protecting people from mosquitoes as untreated nets. Insecticide-treated nets need retreatment each year or every few years, depending on the insecticide used. Some companies have started to make bed nets with insecticides embedded within their fibers, but these nets are not widely available in malarial areas.

Insecticide-treated nets work in three ways. First, the insecticide kills some mosquitoes within a few minutes. Second, the insecticide repels many of the mosquitoes that it does not kill. Third, like an untreated net, the net forms a barrier between the mosquito and the sleeper.

An insecticide-treated bed net costs ten dollars or less. But even that price is too high for many millions of people. When possible, governments and other organizations pass out free nets to those in need. For example, in 2009–2010, UNICEF distributed 5.5 million bed nets in two provinces in the African nation of Democratic Republic of Congo. Some health clinics provide nets to pregnant women and to mothers who bring in their children for vaccinations.

In malarial areas, one person may receive one thousand bites from infected mosquitoes each year. Using nets can slash that number dramatically. The nets are proven lifesavers. For example, Kenya cut child deaths from malaria by 40 percent in just five years by handing out insecticide-treated nets. Still, millions of people around the world don't have bed nets. "We are watching children die—our children—and they die every day," says Stephen Magesa, a scientist with Tanzania's National Institute for Medical Research. "You could save between thirty and fifty per cent of them with nets alone."

Nets don't always reach their intended destinations. Sometimes, corrupt government officials keep donated nets for themselves or sell them instead of distributing them as they're supposed to. Sometimes, it's hard to get nets to people who need them. Some countries have few or poor roads between rural areas and the city or only rutted dirt paths. In addition, gasoline for delivery vehicles is very expensive.

BED NETS FOR ALL

Many groups are working to provide insecticide-treated nets for African children. Schoolchildren, teens, and well-known athletes are helping out. Here are some examples:

- British soccer star David Beckham helped sponsor the purchase of bed nets for the organization Malaria No More.
- NBA all-stars Joe Johnson, Mike Miller, and Jason Kapono shot baskets for dollars, with the donations going to Nothing But Nets.
- Fifth-grade students at Dayton Elementary School in Dayton, Nevada, raised money for nets after reading an article about malaria in *Weekly Reader*.
- Seventh-grade students at Chandler Woods Academy in Belmont, Michigan, started collecting money for nets after studying malaria in Africa.
- A group of elementary school students in Texarkana, Texas, sold cookies and lemonade to pay for mosquito nets.
- Teens at Merritt Island High School in Merritt Island, Florida, added five dollars to the cost of each ticket to their homecoming dance to help pay for nets.
- Sixteen-year-old Emily Fuller of Lake Oswego High School in Lake Oswego, Oregon, set up a table near her school cafeteria, draped it with a mosquito net, and talked to students about malaria. She collected several hundred dollars to purchase bed nets. Former First Lady Laura Bush praised Emily's success at the 2006 White House Summit on Malaria.
- Texas A&M University men's and women's basketball teams raised eight thousand dollars for bed nets at a fund-raiser. The Bill and Melinda Gates Foundation matched donations dollar for dollar.
- Second-grader Katherine Commale of Downington, Pennsylvania, helped her church raise eighty-five thousand dollars for bed nets.

When nets do arrive, people don't always use them. In warm, humid climates, bed nets make hot, sticky nights seem even hotter and stickier. So some people don't hang them up. Only one-fourth to one-half of African children at risk for malaria sleep under bed nets, although that number is increasing.

Sometimes people don't use bed nets for their intended purpose. For instance, some people view the nets as charms to ward off illness and bad luck. They might hide them under their sleeping mats in their original packaging. Others sell their donated bed nets for desperately needed money. Still others use them as fishing nets, as kitchen strainers, and even as decorative trim on wedding dresses. Part of the challenge in protecting people from malaria is educating them about the importance and proper use of bed nets.

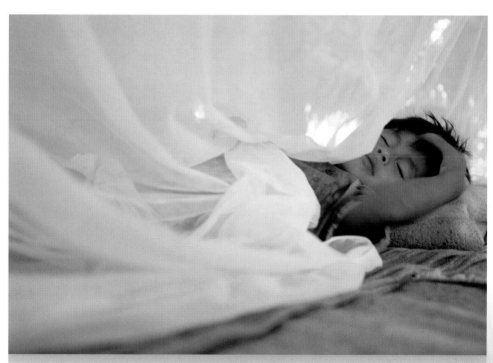

A young boy in Peru sleeps under a bed net. Bed nets are an important tool in keeping malaria from spreading from mosquitoes to humans.

Environmental Controls

In the twenty-first century, public health officials use a variety of approaches to controlling *Anopheles* mosquitoes. Eliminating the standing water where mosquitoes breed is the first approach.

Mosquitoes lay their eggs in freshwater as well as in brackish (slightly salty) water. The body of water may be an irrigation ditch, a pond, a swamp, a rice paddy, or a puddle. It can be water collected in an old tire, a children's wading pool, a birdbath, a fountain, an animal watering trough, a gutter, or even an empty soda can tossed along a highway or hiking path.

The fact that mosquitoes must lay their eggs in water instead of in trees, for example, gives officials a good opportunity to control them. Workers can drain pools of standing water, cover them up, or fill them with dirt. Homeowners can change the water in birdbaths every few days and clean up trash that might hold enough water for mosquitoes to use. The United States wiped out malaria largely by draining hundreds of thousands of acres of standing water.

Not all water can be drained, so people often use chemicals to control mosquitoes. Chemicals designed to kill adult mosquitoes (and other insects) are called insecticides. Those used to kill larvae are called larvicides.

Treating water with larvicides greatly reduces the population of adult mosquitoes. As a result, malaria and other mosquito-borne diseases spread more slowly. Chemicals used to control larvae include:

- Methoprene. People spray methoprene over large bodies of water using helicopters or airplanes. The U.S.

Environmental Protection Agency (EPA) states that the product is safe for humans and does little harm to fish, bees, and other animals.

- Temephos. People put this chemical in water where mosquito larvae live. It is more harmful to plants and animals than other larvicides, so the EPA recommends limiting its use to areas where other methods do not work.

- Monomolecular films. People also put these larvicides in water. The chemicals spread out to form a very thin film on the surface of the water. The film makes it hard for mosquito larvae and pupae to break the water's surface and breathe. They drift downward into the water and drown. The films are safe for humans and pose little risk to other creatures.

- Petroleum-based oils. These oils float on the water's surface and also keep larvae and pupae from breathing. They do not harm humans but may harm some aquatic creatures, such as fish and insects.

- Chlorine in swimming pools. Chlorine repels mosquitoes, keeping them from breeding in pool water. Untreated pools are likely to attract mosquitoes.

Many insecticides kill adult mosquitoes. These insecticides include malathion and pyrethrin. Pyrethrin comes from chrysanthemums, a kind of flower. People also make synthetic pyrethrin in laboratories. Pyrethrin attacks the nervous systems of insects but is not toxic (poisonous) to mammals and birds.

Experts say that most insecticides are not harmful to people. But people must carefully consider whether to use insecticides, especially over large areas, because they may harm the environment. For example, pyrethrin can harm fish. In addition, some insecticides can kill beneficial insects (those that help people by providing food or helping plants grow, such as honeybees) along with killing mosquitoes. Additionally, mosquitoes in some parts of the world are becoming resistant to many insecticides.

Workers usually spread insecticides over wide areas using airplanes. They might use trucks to spray insecticides in specific neighborhoods. For malarial areas of Africa, WHO recommends a mosquito-control technique called indoor residual spraying. This technique involves spraying long-acting insecticides on inside and outside walls and on the roofs of houses.

This man sprays a home in Sudan to protect residents against mosquitoes.

THE DDT DILEMMA

The insecticide DDT is spectacularly successful at killing mosquitoes. Widespread DDT spraying in the 1940s and 1950s helped wipe out malaria in the United States. Other countries also used DDT, with excellent results.

However, by the 1960s, scientific evidence showed that DDT was harmful to the environment. In 1962 U.S. biologist Rachel Carson published an influential book titled *Silent Spring*. In it, she attacked the use of DDT. In addition to killing mosquitoes, the chemical kills many helpful insects, such as bees, butterflies, dragonflies, and praying mantises. DDT also harms seals and many birds, especially peregrine falcons and other raptors (birds of prey). It weakens the birds' eggshells, causing them to break easily.

Because of DDT, some bird populations declined greatly in the mid-twentieth century. By the 1970s, scientists counted fewer than 325 nesting pairs of peregrines in the United States. The United States and most other countries banned DDT in the 1970s.

With the resurgence of mosquitoes and malaria since then, some countries are taking a second look at DDT. It is six times cheaper than alternative insecticides. One spraying lasts nearly nine months. In 2007 WHO approved the limited use of DDT for indoor residual spraying worldwide. Using DDT only indoors lessens the risk to wildlife. Yet some research suggests that DDT may concentrate in human breast milk and that it may cause cancer. Other reports find that risk to be very small.

The use of DDT is creating a lot of controversy. Global public health officials are trying to balance saving lives through DDT use with possible long-term harm to the environment and human health. We don't yet know the long-term effects of indoor residual spraying on people.

Anopheles gambiae prefers to be indoors with humans. After feeding, female *Anopheles gambiae* must rest on walls, often for several hours. Indoor residual spraying takes advantage of this situation. Although indoor spraying doesn't help people who've already been bitten, killing mosquitoes after feeding breaks the continued mosquito-to-person transmission cycle. Most experts consider indoor residual spraying safe for people, although some experts question its safety over the long term.

Indoor residual spraying can be extremely effective. In one malaria-control program in Asia and South America, it reduced malaria cases by 90 percent. And because indoor residual spraying occurs only in and around human dwellings, it is less harmful to the environment than insecticides sprayed across fields and forests. However, poverty and poor public health systems prevent wide use of the method in Africa, where it is most needed.

Chemicals aren't the only way to control the mosquito population. People also use bacteria and other living things to control mosquitoes and their larvae. *Bacillus thuringiensis israelensis (Bti)* is a bacterium that grows naturally in the soil. When mosquito larvae eat the bacteria, toxins in the *Bti* kill the larvae. Another natural larvicide is *Bacillus sphaericus (B. sphaericus)*, a bacterium that is common around the world. Extensive testing suggests that *Bti* and *B. sphaericus* harm only their targets—mosquito larvae— and not other living things. To get the bacteria to the larvae, people mix them with fluids and spray the mixture over crops and waterways. While effective, bacteria-based larvicides are not yet widely used in malaria-prone regions because they are more expensive than other available larvicides.

Scientists have long known that "mosquito fish" love to

eat a few dozen mosquito larvae for lunch. Another name for the mosquito fish is *Gambusia*. Only 1 to 3 inches (2.5 to 8 centimeters) long, each *Gambusia* eats about one hundred larvae or pupae per day. In Ghana, Somalia, Sudan, Pakistan, Thailand, India, and other countries, governments routinely stock ponds and lakes with mosquito fish.

In parts of Africa, people are stocking abandoned fishponds, ditches, and other waterlogged areas with a larvae-eating fish called the Nile tilapia. In an experiment in Kenya, researchers drained stagnant ponds and filled them with clean water and tilapia. Within weeks, the adult mosquito population in the region fell by 94 percent. An edible fish, the tilapia grows to be 2 feet (0.6 m) long. This useful fish not only wipes out mosquitoes but can also feed people.

Gambusia, or mosquito fish, eat mosquito larvae. Some countries stock ponds with this fish to help control the mosquito population.

Another useful biological tool in the fight against malaria is a spider named *Evarcha culicivora*. This spider lives only around Lake Victoria in Kenya and Uganda. The spider hunts its prey by sight and smell. When offered a variety of mosquitoes and other insects, the spider always chooses the female *Anopheles*. Health officials in the Lake Victoria region tell residents to leave these spiders alone so they can eat mosquitoes.

Preventive Medications

Health officials in many countries recommend that people take medications to prevent malaria or to decrease its severity. WHO and other international health organizations strongly support this practice.

WHO recommends that all pregnant women living in areas of endemic malaria receive two to three preventive doses of an antimalarial drug, generally between the twentieth and thirty-fifth week of pregnancy. (A normal pregnancy is forty weeks.) This approach is called intermittent preventive treatment. A study in Malawi showed that among women who took this treatment, parasitic infection of the placenta dropped by nearly one-third. The women gave birth to nearly 25 percent fewer low-birth-weight babies. Two or three doses of intermittent preventive treatment will not cure malaria, but they can greatly decrease the number of malaria parasites in the mother's body. This decrease ensures a healthier baby.

The same treatment works well for infants. In some places, doctors give babies intermittent preventive treatment at two, three, and nine months of age, even if they are not known to have malaria. This treatment reduces malaria and anemia in the first year of life by 60 percent.

Doctors use preventive treatment mainly for infants, children, and young women who are pregnant or may become pregnant. Men and older women generally don't need to take preventive medications. When foreigners travel to malarial areas for business or vacation, doctors often prescribe preventive medications before, during, and after travel.

All drugs have the potential for serious side effects. Antimalarial medications are no exception. Side effects can include nausea, vomiting, anxiety, fatigue, confusion, ringing in the ears, headaches, and seizures. Most people, however, have few problems after taking antimalaria medication.

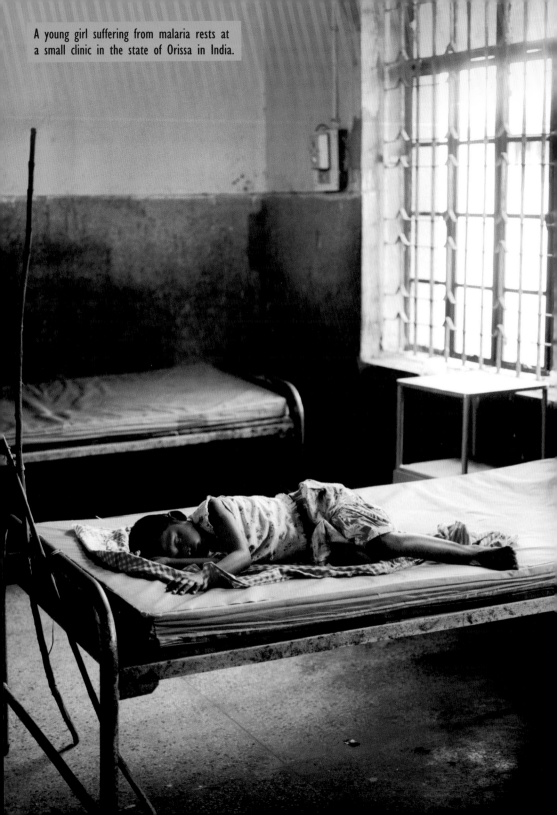

A young girl suffering from malaria rests at a small clinic in the state of Orissa in India.

DIAGNOSING AND TREATING MALARIA

According to medical books, the classic malaria attack lasts six to ten hours and consists of three stages:

- The cold stage. The infected person feels intense cold and shivers. Chills and shivers are the body's way of generating heat by muscle twitches. Even though people with chills feel terribly cold, the chills signal that the body's temperature is on the rise.

- The hot stage. The infected person has a high fever and headaches. The body is trying to kill off the parasites with heat. This works fairly well with certain bacterial and viral infections. But malaria parasites are resistant to increased body heat. A higher body temperature has little effect on them.

- The wet stage. The infected person sweats profusely. The sweating is a sign that the fever has broken. It is the body's attempt to cool off and return to a normal temperature.

In reality, most people experience a jumble of symptoms: shaking, chills, high fevers, drenching sweats, bad headaches, nausea, vomiting, diarrhea, body aches, and severe fatigue. Without treatment, the symptoms can occur on an average cycle of every three days with *P. malariae* and every two days with the other parasites.

The first attack occurs when the schizont, the stage of the parasite that matures in the liver, ruptures and releases merozoites into the bloodstream. Fever, chills, and other symptoms are part of the body's immune response to the invading merozoites. The merozoites find and enter red blood cells within minutes. Once the merozoites are inside, the body's immune system cannot reach them. A person with malaria may feel slightly better at this point, except for extreme fatigue.

The next malaria attack occurs a few days later, when new merozoites burst from red blood cells. Once more, the body's immune system swings into attack mode with chills and fever. But patients with only chills and fever are the lucky ones. The situation can get much worse.

The most dangerous and deadly form of malaria, caused by *P. falciparum*, produces the sickest patients. The parasite can cause severe anemia as it gobbles up oxygen-bearing hemoglobin. In people infected by *P. falciparum*, hemoglobin can fall to half the normal level. The lack of hemoglobin in the bloodstream starves the body of oxygen. No matter how fast the person breathes, the lungs and heart cannot deliver enough oxygen to the body when the hemoglobin is extremely low.

In addition to anemia, other malaria symptoms might include swelling of the liver and spleen, kidney failure, blood clotting problems, bleeding into the brain or kidneys, low blood sugar, falling blood pressure, and shock.

But even these conditions are not the worst-case scenario. That dubious distinction falls to cerebral malaria. A normal red blood cell has a smooth, flexible, disklike shape that allows it to squeeze through capillaries, the body's tiniest blood vessels. Infection with *P. falciparum* changes the red blood cell into a rigid, round shape with knobs. When infected red blood cells circulate through capillaries in the brain, their sticky, Velcro-like knobs latch onto the inside of the capillaries. Holed up in the red blood cells, the parasites can hang out in the capillaries of the brain until the merozoites mature.

People with cerebral malaria are critically ill. The infected blood cells block the brain capillaries, depriving the brain cells of oxygen. The brain starts to swell. Within a day or so, a patient can go from having simple fevers and chills to having seizures. He or she may fall into a coma. In the worst cases, cerebral malaria can kill within twenty-four hours.

On average, one of every five children with cerebral malaria dies from it. Between 10 and 25 percent of the survivors have permanent neurological (nervous system) damage, such as blindness, speech disorders, and problems moving arms and legs. These children may never walk or speak normally. Other survivors may experience behavioral problems and learning difficulties. These problems can affect children for the rest of their lives.

Diagnosing Malaria

In areas of endemic malaria, people usually assume that a child with chills and a fever has malaria. Many other diseases cause similar symptoms, but parents and health-care workers think of malaria first, because it is so common. When doctors suspect malaria, they usually do tests to be sure. The sooner treatment starts, the better the chances of a complete recovery. There are several ways to diagnose malaria:

Microscope

To diagnose malaria with a microscope, a health worker takes a small sample of blood from the patient. A simple pinprick of the finger is enough. Because babies' fingers are so tiny, health workers stick babies on the heel instead.

A laboratory worker smears the blood onto a glass slide and stains it with a chemical. The chemical makes the parasites easier to see. The worker places the stained slide under a microscope and examines the red blood cells for signs of parasites. The parasites appear blue with a red spot inside them.

A blood sample from an infected person may show no parasites—especially if only a small number of blood cells are infected. So if someone seems to have malaria but the first blood test is negative (does not show malaria parasites), workers will usually repeat the test to make sure.

If the test is positive, the lab worker estimates the percentage of infected red blood cells. In the sickest patients, 25 to 30 percent of the cells might be infected. The more infected red blood cells a person has, the sicker he or she will be.

Microscopic diagnosis of malaria is the most common method. It's highly reliable and relatively cheap, other than the initial cost of the microscope. But the method has a few drawbacks. Some lab workers don't have the training they

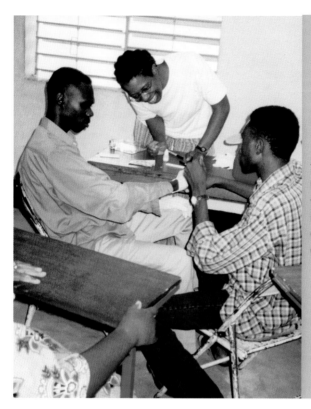

This doctor trains local physicians in western Africa on how to use a rapid diagnostic test to detect malaria.

need. The staining chemicals can go bad in the tropical heat. The best microscopes need electricity or batteries for proper use. These are not always readily available in many parts of the world.

Rapid Diagnostic Tests (RDTs)

In these tests, a health worker smears a small amount of a patient's blood on a testing card or dipstick. The test determines if malaria antigens are present in the blood. Antigens are proteins on parasites, bacteria, and viruses that stimulate the body to form antibodies. If malaria antigens are present, the patient is infected with malaria. The test gives results in only ten to fifteen minutes.

About forty types of RDTs are available. Some RDTs can tell which parasite is causing the infection. This information is important because treatment may vary according to the kind of parasite. Experts recommend that health workers follow up RDTs with microscopic testing when possible.

RDTs cost more than microscopic testing, but people can use them when no microscopes are available. In addition, health workers need little training to use them correctly. Some countries—Uganda, for example—provide RDTs for people to test themselves for malaria at home. If a test is positive, a person can seek treatment right away.

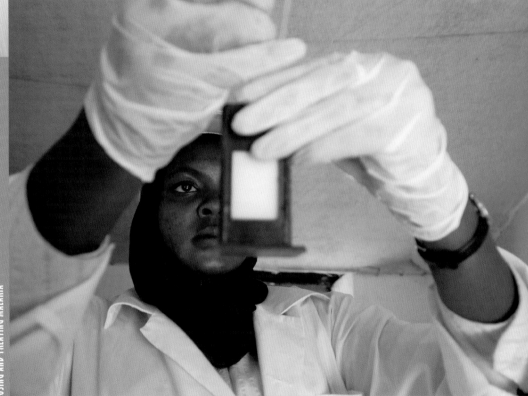

A laboratory technician checks a blood sample for malaria at a refugee camp in West Darfur, Sudan.

Polymerase chain reaction (PCR) is a test that detects genetic material called deoxyribonucleic acid (DNA) in malaria parasites. The test collects a tiny sample of DNA and duplicates it. Duplication provides enough DNA for examination. PCR is the most reliable malaria test. It can detect very low levels of infection that cannot be detected by other methods. But the test involves high-tech equipment. It is expensive and not widely available, especially in poor countries.

Health workers can also test blood for the presence of malaria antibodies. Antibodies can take several weeks to form, so the antibody test will not spot a brand-new infection. And malaria antibodies remain in the body for life. So an antibody test will be positive if a person has ever had malaria—even if he or she does not currently have it. This limits the usefulness of the test.

Doctors can diagnose cerebral malaria by looking into a patient's eyes using an instrument called an ophthalmoscope. With an ophthalmoscope, a doctor can see bleeding into a part of the eye called the retina. The doctor can also see swelling of the optic nerve. This bleeding and swelling happen with malaria and a number of other diseases. But malaria produces unique white patches and whitened blood vessels in the back of the eye. Their presence is a sure sign of cerebral malaria.

Treating Malaria

Malaria is curable when patients take the right medications at the right dosage for the right length of time. But many people don't get the correct medication, dosage, or course of treatment. In many countries, people cannot afford malaria medication, which can cost up to ten dollars per day.

A doctor has a lot to consider before giving medications to malaria patients. A doctor must ask the following questions:

- Which parasite is the likely cause? *P. falciparum* might call for different medications than the other three parasites. Patients with *P. vivax* and *P. ovale* may need additional treatment to rid the liver of dormant parasites, so that the malaria does not recur years later.

- How old is the patient? Babies and young children cannot take certain medications. Doctors must also carefully calculate dosages based on a person's weight.

- If the patient is female, is she pregnant? A pregnant woman cannot take some medications because they damage the fetus.

- Is the malaria parasite resistant to certain medications? Resistance to common antimalaria medications is a growing problem. Giving a useless medication wastes time and money and may even harm a patient.

- How sick is the patient?

- Does the patient have any other conditions along with the malaria, such as HIV infection or tuberculosis? Coexisting medical conditions will affect the choice of antimalaria medications.

WHO carefully monitors malaria around the world. It recommends specific medications in each country. Some

Bruce joined the U.S. Peace Corps (PC) when he was twenty-one. He worked in the west African nation of Liberia for two years. He took chloroquine, the medication that was supposed to keep him from getting malaria.

"Even though I took my meds, I nearly died from malaria out in a remote village," Bruce says. "Fortunately, someone called in another Peace Corps volunteer from a nearby village. He took me to his hut and dumped buckets of cold well water on me all night long to break my high fever. That probably saved my life. In three days, I felt well enough to ride my motorcycle 100 miles [160 km] on muddy dirt roads until I reached the larger village where the other PC volunteers stayed.

"When I got to the village, I collapsed and got a lot worse. A few days later a PC nurse drove me to a clinic for treatment. At the clinic the doctors gave me a variety of pills and shots and dripped fluids into my veins to rehydrate me. The place was overflowing with people, young and old, who were even worse off than me. By the time I was cured of my malaria, I'd lost 20 pounds [9 kilograms]."

medications can both prevent malaria and treat it. Important medications in the treatment of malaria include:

Quinine-Based Medications

Quinine originally came from the bark of the *Cinchona* tree, the "fever tree" of South America. People later successfully grew *Cinchona* trees on plantations (large farms) in India, Java, and Sri Lanka. They made quinine from parts of the tree's bark, roots, and branches. While quinine does not "cure" malaria, it kills enough malaria parasites that a patient's own immune system can kill the rest.

Chloroquine, a synthetic form of quinine, was the most widely used quinine-based medication for decades. It was spectacularly successful at treating malaria. But throughout the 1980s and 1990s, the dangerous *P. falciparum* parasite became increasingly resistant to chloroquine. Resistance appeared first in parts of Asia and South America and then in Africa.

Scientists have developed dozens of medications based on chloroquine. *P. falciparum* is susceptible to each for a time. Then the parasite develops resistance. Few places

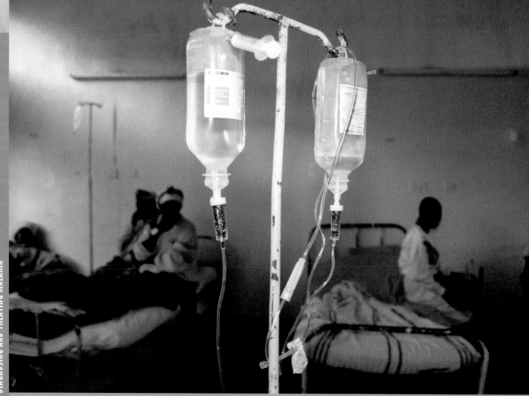

DIAGNOSING AND TREATING MALARIA

These patients are being treated for malaria in a hospital in Kenya.

remain where malaria caused by *P. falciparum* responds to chloroquine or another quinine-based medication. Chloroquine still works against *P. ovale*, *P. vivax*, and *P. malariae* in many parts of the world, however.

Antibiotics

Antibiotics are powerful medications used to treat infections caused by bacteria. Most antibiotics have little effect on malaria or other diseases caused by parasites. However, a few antibiotics are effective against malaria.

An important treatment for malaria is a combination drug called SP. It contains the antibiotic sulfadoxine and the drug pyrimethamine. Doctors sometimes combine SP with the quinine-based drug amodiaquine (AQ). They use the combination in regions where malaria parasites are not resistant to these drugs. Many countries started using SP alone or SP plus AQ as quinine-based medications became less effective.

Artemisinin

Artemisinin-based medications are both the oldest and the newest treatments for malaria. In an ancient medical text, the Chinese wrote about using the qinghao plant to treat fevers. The Chinese used this herb, also known as sweet wormwood, for more than two thousand years. The rest of the world didn't discover it until modern times.

During the 1970s, malaria became a major problem in parts of China. In 1971 Chinese scientists identified the active ingredient in sweet wormwood as artemisinin. In the 1990s, scientists found a very similar plant, *Artemesia annua*, in the United States. In the twenty-first century, artemisinin-based medications are the most powerful antimalaria medications in the world.

Artemisinin-based drugs are very effective against malaria. They are extremely valuable where malaria has become resistant to quinine-based medications. Doctors usually give artemisinin medications in combination with one or more other antimalaria drugs. This process is called artemisinin combination therapy, or ACT. By giving two or more antimalaria medications together, the chance of the parasite developing resistance to any one of them greatly decreases.

Many countries in Africa, Southeast Asia, and South America use ACT as a first-line treatment for malaria. ACT is proving very successful. For example, Zambia once lost up to fifty thousand children each year to malaria. The widespread use of ACT has reduced the childhood death rate by one-third.

In just a few years, the demand for ACT has increased dramatically. Paying for these medications strains the public health systems of poor nations. Old medications such as chloroquine cost about ten cents per treatment per day. But ACT drugs may cost several dollars per day, a very large amount for people who live in poverty.

To increase artemisinin supplies, farmers in Tanzania and other African nations have started to grow sweet wormwood. With more artemisinin, the cost of artemisinin-based medications may decrease.

Supportive Care

Health workers also treat malaria patients with supportive care. This care includes medications to reduce fever, lessen pain, and control seizures. People with severe malaria can become dehydrated. They lose a lot of body fluids when they sweat. In addition, sick people often cannot drink enough fluids because of nausea or weakness. So supportive care also includes giving fluids intravenously (through the veins). The intravenous fluids are mixtures of water, sugar, and salt.

The sickest patients may need blood transfusions to replace red blood cells destroyed by malaria parasites. People with damaged kidneys may need dialysis—treatments to cleanse the blood. Children with cerebral malaria may be unconscious and may need ventilators, machines to help them breathe.

Failure and Success

Throughout Africa, Asia, and Latin America, huge numbers of people do not have access to such advanced medical care, especially in rural areas. Instead, they travel to small clinics for basic care. Some people with malaria do not get any medical care at all. They stay at home while worried family members do what they can to make them feel a little better. Without medical care, many young children do not survive malaria.

Despite these obstacles, health-care leaders point to some successes. For example, in one district in Zanzibar (part of Tanzania), ACT reduced by half the number of children with malaria parasites in their blood. Adding insecticide-treated bed nets to ACT decreased the number of children with malaria parasites in their blood by 90 percent. ACT and insecticide-treated nets also reduced hospital admissions and malaria deaths by 75 percent. The success of appropriate medications and widespread use of bed nets shows that people can control malaria, if not wipe it out.

THE PROBLEM OF FAKE DRUGS

Just as people can buy cheap counterfeit designer clothing and handbags, they can also buy fake drugs. Counterfeit malaria medications are flooding Asia and Africa. In one sampling of malaria medicine in Southeast Asia, more than half turned out to be fake. Most of the phony medicine is made in China, India, and Pakistan. The business of making and selling fake malaria drugs is worth billions of dollars.

In many parts of the world, people buy malaria medicines from pharmacies or street vendors. They don't need a doctor's prescription to buy the drugs. Other people get malaria medications free from clinics or hospitals, which in turn get the medications free from governments or charitable organizations. If the governments, organizations, and pharmacies buy medications from reputable drugmakers, the medications will be effective. But not all drugmakers and sellers are honest. Sometimes charities and health organizations unknowingly buy counterfeit drugs and deliver them to patients. One charity working in Myanmar unknowingly bought one hundred thousand tablets of fake artemisinin.

The most obvious problem with fake malaria drugs is that people who take them aren't getting proper treatment. They may die instead of being cured. Dora Akunyili, head of the agency that controls drug safety in Nigeria, says, "Drug counterfeiting is mass murder. It is one of the greatest atrocities of our time."

But that is not the only problem. Some fake drugs contain

small amounts of artemisinin—just enough to make the patient feel a little better. These weak drugs kill only the weakest malaria parasites. The stronger parasites survive to reproduce. They pass their drug resistance on to the next generation. Malaria parasites are already resistant to the older drugs chloroquine and SP. In some parts of the world, the artemisinin family of drugs is the only weapon left in the fight against malaria. If the parasites become widely resistant to those medications, it's uncertain what drugs, if any, will be able to take their place.

Some fake drugs contain acetaminophen (brand name Tylenol), which helps fever and pain but does not cure malaria. Others contain chloroquine, which helps fever and pain but no longer cures malaria in most regions. Still other drugs contain sulfa, an antibiotic that can cause severe reactions in people who are allergic to it.

In some cases, dishonest sellers buy expired malaria drugs—which are too old to be effective—and repackage them with new expiration dates and resell them. Some fake drugs have no medicine at all. They are made entirely of starch, chalk, flour, or sugar. They may even be contaminated with harmful substances.

People can use test kits to determine if a malaria medication is real. Testers mix a chemical with a tiny bit of the pill. If an artemisinin-based drug is in the pill, the chemical turns yellow. However, the tests don't show how much of the drug is in the pill or if it is still effective.

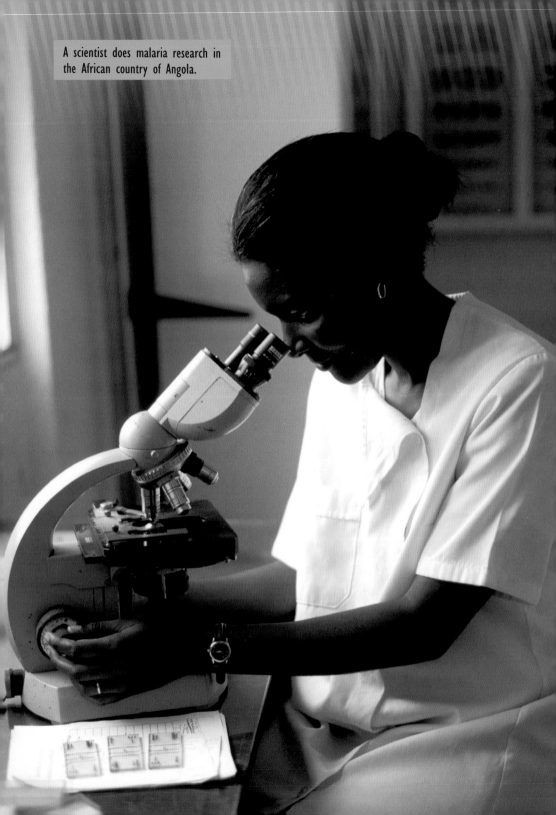

A scientist does malaria research in the African country of Angola.

Chapter 8

THE FUTURE OF MALARIA

Worldwide efforts to eradicate malaria began in the 1940s and wound down in the 1970s. As malaria has come roaring back around the world, people have geared up to fight the disease once again. Much of the work takes place in scientific laboratories. Some scientists are studying mosquitoes and the *Plasmodium* parasite. Others are working on vaccines and new medications.

Building a Better Mosquito

Much research focuses on mosquitoes and the *Plasmodium* parasite. The parasite is almost as harmful to mosquitoes as it is to people. If scientists could keep mosquitoes from becoming infected with *Plasmodium*, they could also keep people from getting malaria. Scientists at the Johns Hopkins Malaria Research Institute in Baltimore, Maryland, are working toward this goal. The scientists identified a previously unknown mosquito antigen. The malaria parasite uses this antigen to enter the mosquito's gut. Scientists created antibodies to this antigen. The scientists then inserted the antibodies into mosquitoes to help them fight off the parasite.

These mosquitoes with the antibodies are called transgenic mosquitoes. When natural mosquitoes and transgenic mosquitoes feasted on malaria-infected mice, the transgenic mosquitoes had a better survival rate than did the natural mosquitoes. Six days after feeding, malaria had killed more than half of the natural mosquitoes, while only one-third of the transgenic mosquitoes had died. The new antibody had partially protected the transgenic mosquitoes from the malaria parasite.

What's more, the transgenic mosquitoes were healthier than the natural mosquitoes because they were not weakened by malaria. When natural and transgenic mosquitoes bred, the healthier, transgenic mosquitoes laid more eggs. After a few generations of captive breeding, transgenic mosquitoes made up about 70 percent of the resulting population.

At a laboratory in France, a scientist studies mosquitoes that carry malaria.

People can never totally wipe out mosquitoes. But one day, scientists may release large numbers of malaria-resistant transgenic mosquitoes into the wild. Soon the malaria-resistant mosquitoes would make up most of the mosquito population of a region. Fewer mosquitoes would carry the malaria parasite, and fewer people would get malaria.

Humans versus Mosquitoes

Scientists are also looking for new ways to repel and kill mosquitoes and ways to keep them from reproducing. In one promising study, scientists discovered the maxillary palp. This sensory organ sticks out of the head of the *Anopheles gambiae*. It contains receptor cells that are sensitive to chemicals in human breath and sweat. The mosquito uses the organ to locate humans. The discovery may lead to the development of improved mosquito repellents that block the mosquito's ability to detect human body odors.

Scientists have also identified the genes that allow mosquitoes to find people by the smell of our sweat. One day we may repel mosquitoes using special deodorants—antimosquito antiperspirant—that inactivate those genes.

Male mosquitoes "sing" to female mosquitoes by flapping their wings at specific speeds before mating. (This singing is the mosquitoes' characteristic buzzing sound.) Some males sing better than others. The good singers are the ones that mate with the females. Scientists hope to breed better male singers that are also sterile, or infertile. Once released into the wild, the sterile males would mate with females, but the females wouldn't produce fertile eggs.

For years U.S. farmers have used a fungus called *Beauveria bassiana* to kill aphids and termites. The fungus is harmless to humans. Researchers believe that bed nets treated with this fungus or other fungi could work as well against mosquitoes as nets treated with insecticides. The fungi-treated nets would be safer for people. Even better, mosquitoes do not seem to become resistant to fungi as they do to insecticides.

A type of bacterium called *Wolbachia* infects many insects, although not usually mosquitoes. Australian scientists have discovered a way to infect mosquitoes with *Wolbachia*. The bacterium cuts a mosquito's life span in half. If people could infect large mosquito populations with *Wolbachia*, the insects would die within days—before they could reproduce.

Plasmodium Research

Some scientists are studying *Plasmodium* and how it sickens people. For instance, Swedish researchers are learning how malaria parasites make red blood cells knobby and sticky. This stickiness causes infected cells to clog capillaries in the brain, lungs, and kidneys. One day medications may prevent this stickiness, decreasing the number of cases of cerebral malaria.

German scientists are investigating how malaria parasites move from liver cells to red blood cells while avoiding the human immune system. They've discovered that the parasites disguise the antigens that would normally trigger the immune system to swing into action. If scientists can learn how to block this cloaking process, the immune system would be better able to recognize the parasites and attack them while still in the bloodstream.

Researchers are also investigating exactly how *P. falciparum* developed resistance to chloroquine. Resistance arose in several parts of the world at nearly the same time. This study may help keep mosquitoes from developing resistance to future medications.

Meanwhile, researchers at Georgetown University Medical Center in Washington, D.C., have constructed an artificial *Plasmodium*-like gene. The gene, which took two years to build, allows scientists to study how the malaria parasite becomes resistant to medications.

Finally, scientists are developing PCR tests to screen for *Plasmodium* DNA in people's urine and saliva, rather than in their blood. This method is easier than collecting blood with needles. It's also safer in places where medical supplies are scarce, because reused needles can spread diseases such as HIV/AIDS and hepatitis C, as well as malaria.

New Malaria Drugs

Many researchers are looking for better drug treatments for people with malaria. In many parts of the world, artemisinin-based medications are the only ones that work consistently. Experts hope the parasites will not develop resistance to those important drugs in the near future, but it is likely to happen at some point. So the continued search for new antimalaria medications is vital.

Researchers at Johns Hopkins University are developing a promising drug. The drug is based on peroxide compounds and mimics the active ingredient in artemisinin. Normally, malaria parasites digest hemoglobin from red blood cells. This process releases a substance called heme. The meeting of heme and peroxide creates a powerful chemical reaction that kills the parasite. The new peroxide-based drug appears to be far safer than many other malaria treatments. It cures malaria-infected mice with just one dose. Scientists started testing testing the peroxide-based drug on humans in 2010.

Scientists at the University of California at Berkeley have used genetic engineering in the search for new malaria medicine. (Genetic engineering is the changing of genetic material to produce a new type of organism.) The scientists have developed a strain of yeast that produces large amounts of synthetic artemisinin. Drug companies plan to start producing the synthetic artemisinin on a large scale in early 2011. The medicine will cost pennies per dose instead of dollars. In addition to being cheaper than artemisinin made from sweet wormwood, the new medicine will be easier to produce. Drugmakers will not have to worry about problems such as bad weather and political unrest, which sometimes disrupt the planting, harvesting, and processing of sweet wormwood.

A few other medicines are also under study. For instance, scientists in Portugal have cured mice dying of cerebral malaria with carbon monoxide. The gas bonds with hemoglobin to prevent its destruction by malaria parasites. But carbon monoxide is a highly toxic gas. It might not be safe to give to humans. Finally, most available medications work against the stages of the malaria parasite that live in the bloodstream. But a drug called tazopsine—derived from a plant that grows in Madagascar—is proving effective against the parasite's liver stage.

Vaccine Research

Scientists have been searching for a malaria vaccine since the late twentieth century. Creating such a vaccine is very difficult because of the parasite's dual hosts—human and mosquito—and its many stages within those hosts. Nonetheless, dozens of malaria vaccine projects are under way. Each project targets a different part of the parasite's life cycle. Some experimental vaccines exist only in the laboratory. Others are being tested on small groups of people.

One of the most promising vaccines is called RTS,S. In 2008 doctors gave it to several hundred babies between the ages of five and seventeen months in Tanzania and Kenya. The vaccine cut the risk of malaria infection by more than one-half during the ten-month trial. Because the results were so promising, doctors decided to test even more people. In May 2009, doctors gave the experimental vaccine to sixteen thousand infants and children in seven African nations.

The RTS,S vaccine is not as effective as other childhood vaccines, such as those for measles and polio. But its results are the best yet achieved by a malaria vaccine. World health officials hope that RTS,S will be widely available for use in infants by 2012 and available for all children under five years old by 2014.

A U.S. company named Sanaria may also be very close to a successful vaccine. (*Sanaria* means "healthy air"—the opposite of *malaria*, or "bad air.") In the company's Maryland laboratory, researchers feed human blood infected with *P. falciparum* to mosquitoes. The researchers then zap the infected mosquitoes with enough radiation to weaken—but not kill—the parasites. Technicians remove the mosquitoes' salivary glands, where up to one hundred thousand radiated parasites hide out. The technicians then turn the weakened parasites into an experimental vaccine.

The best way to prevent a disease is with vaccination. Doctors routinely vaccinate children against such childhood diseases as measles, chicken pox, diphtheria, polio, tetanus, and mumps. With widespread vaccination, these once-common diseases have become rare in many countries. The bad news is that scientists have not yet succeeded in creating a vaccine to prevent malaria—although several are in various stages of testing. Here's why creating a *Plasmodium* vaccine is so difficult:

- *Complexity.* To create a vaccine, scientists must understand an organism's genetic makeup. The polio virus has eleven genes. The influenza (flu) virus has eight. By comparison, *P. falciparum* has more than five thousand genes, which makes understanding it very difficult.

- *Constant motion.* The malaria parasite is constantly on the run. In a process repeated over and over, it moves from a mosquito to the human bloodstream, where it lingers for just minutes before heading to the liver. Then it heads to the red blood cells. Each parasitic stage presents a different challenge for the human immune system.

- *Change.* *P. falciparum* has many strains, or variations. Indeed, each region seems to have its own strain. A single vaccine cannot yet address these many strains. In addition, the parasite is constantly mutating to dodge the human immune system and the medications designed to wipe it out.

A research scientist dissects a mosquito to collect its saliva at Sanaria, a Maryland-based research company.

Getting a dose of this vaccine is like getting bitten by one thousand infected mosquitoes at once. But since the parasites have been weakened, they do not cause malaria. The vaccinated person produces antibodies that are ready to battle the malaria parasite in the future. In tests, the vaccine protected 90 percent of volunteers from developing malaria for nearly one year.

In April 2009, the U.S. Food and Drug Administration gave Sanaria approval to further test the vaccine. Doctors will give it to a small number of adult volunteers to evaluate its safety, determine a safe dosage range, and identify side effects.

Scientists at the National Institutes of Health in Bethesda, Maryland, are working on a vaccine that would kill the malaria parasite in mosquitoes. Vaccinated mosquitoes could no longer pass malaria parasites to people. In tests, the vaccine successfully stopped the spread of malaria in mice.

A SCIENTIST TESTS A MALARIA VACCINE

Stephen Hoffman, a doctor and scientist, heads the U.S. drug company Sanaria. He has spent more than twenty-five years working on a vaccine to prevent malaria. In 1984 he was director of the malaria program at the Naval Medical Research Center in Bethesda, Maryland. Hoffman was certain he'd invented the perfect malaria vaccine. He was so confident in the vaccine that he gave it to himself. Then he let mosquitoes infected with malaria bite him.

The next day, Hoffman flew from Washington, D.C., to San Diego, California, to attend a medical conference and give a talk about his new vaccine. While he was speaking, he felt a wave of coldness flow through him. He staggered to a chair and collapsed. He slumped, shaking with chills and fever, teeth chattering. It didn't take long before Hoffman realized the vaccine was a failure. He had given himself malaria.

How do you vaccinate trillions of mosquitoes? There's no way to do that, of course. Instead, doctors would give the vaccine to humans, even though it's designed to protect mosquitoes. Eating a vaccinated human's blood would vaccinate a mosquito against the *Plasmodium* parasite. Over time, fewer and fewer mosquitoes would carry the parasite.

Researchers at Johns Hopkins University in Baltimore have identified chains of sugar molecules that line the mosquito stomach. These sugar chains let malaria parasites latch on and reproduce inside mosquitoes. Reducing the size of these sugar chains keeps 95 percent of parasites from attaching to the stomachs of mosquitoes and halts their reproduction. One day, a human vaccine passed along to feeding mosquitoes may block the sugar production of mosquitoes and kill malaria parasites.

Bill and Melinda Gates speak about the fight against malaria at the Malaria Forum in Seattle, Washington, in October 2007. The Bill and Melinda Gates Foundation is working to eradicate malaria worldwide.

Roll Back Malaria

Some people in the United States and other wealthy nations pay little attention to malaria because it doesn't affect them. But Bill Gates, the founder of Microsoft Corporation and cofounder of the Bill and Melinda Gates Foundation, wants Americans and others to take a closer look at malaria. Gates said, "If we re-sorted the world and your neighbors [in the United States] were dying of malaria, it would be viewed as a total crisis." Driving the point home, Gates's hometown newspaper, the *Seattle Times*, stresses that malaria kills an African child every thirty seconds. At that rate, malaria would wipe out Seattle's forty-six thousand public school children in about two weeks.

A baby gets tested for malaria at a refugee camp in Thailand.

Since the late twentieth century, the Gates Foundation and international organizations have revitalized the fight against malaria. In 1998 WHO, UNICEF, the United Nations Development Programme, and the World Bank created the Roll Back Malaria Partnership. The partnership includes more than five hundred governments, private organizations, foundations, and research institutes. The partnership has begun a massive effort to bring malaria under control. The Gates Foundation has donated more than one billion dollars to this work.

The partnership has set forth ambitious goals in its Global Malaria Action Plan. This program to wipe out malaria will likely cost $6.2 billion in 2010 and $5.1 billion more each year over the next ten years. Program goals include:

- Providing insecticide-treated nets, spraying households with insecticides, and making appropriate drugs available for all people at risk for malaria

- Reducing malaria cases to 25 percent of 2000 levels by 2015

- Eliminating malaria in eight to ten countries by 2015

- Controlling malaria in the short term and eradicating it completely, country by country, in the long term

The Gates Foundation also partners with other international organizations, including the Malaria Vaccine Initiative; the Global Fund to Fight AIDS, Tuberculosis and Malaria; the Malaria Eradication Research Agenda; and the Global Health Group. In Bill Gates's 2009 annual letter outlining the foundation's work, he stated, "The malaria community has a goal to reduce deaths by over half by 2015, which is aggressive, but it is in line with the results in communities where bed nets and other tools have been rolled out." Eventually, the Gates Foundation, Roll Back Malaria, and other groups hope to see malaria once again brought under control on Earth.

More to Be Done

Experience has shown that malaria can be prevented and controlled. For instance, the widespread use of insecticide-treated bed nets and ACT has reduced childhood malaria deaths by 67 percent in Rwanda and 62 percent in Ethiopia. In Zambia six in ten pregnant women take antimalaria medications during pregnancy, greatly reducing the risk of stillbirth and miscarriage. In some urban areas of Zambia,

People look at mosquito nets for sale in Tanzania. Getting mosquito nets to people in areas stricken with malaria is a major goal of the Bill and Melinda Gates Foundation.

nearly three-quarters of houses are routinely sprayed with insecticide. Half of Zambia's people own one or more insecticide-treated bed nets. Such low-tech measures can greatly reduce the number of malaria deaths. But not everyone who needs these measures can get them.

"Every day, thousands of mothers watch helplessly as their children die from a disease that we have known how to prevent for decades," said Melinda Gates.[25] "The continuing toll of malaria is a moral outrage. We would not allow it here in the United States, and we should not allow it anywhere. The world is finally waking up to the malaria catastrophe. It's time to close the gap in funding, accelerate research, and work together in a more strategic way to strengthen the global malaria fight."

The world seems poised to conquer this killer disease after decades of neglect. Around the globe, national governments, charitable organizations, and individuals are banding together to fight this terrible disease that steals the health and lives of so many. Perhaps someday malaria will become a nuisance ailment—one easily cured with a couple of doses of medication. Or perhaps it will vanish entirely.

TIMELINE

CA. 2550 B.C. Chinese emperor Huang Ti writes about malaria in *Nei Ching*.

CA. 1325 B.C. Ancient Egyptians write about malaria in the *London Medical Papyrus*.

500s B.C. The Indian physician Sushruta describes malaria in *Sushruta Samhita*.

400s B.C. The Greek physician Hippocrates writes about malaria, including its cycle of fever and chills.

200 B.C. Ancient Chinese write about the qinghao plant in *52 Remedies*.

1500s–1600s European explorers and soldiers bring malaria to the Americas.

1632 Italians learn about *Cinchona* bark, which contains quinine, from priests working in South America.

1850s People begin growing *Cinchona* trees in India, Java, and Sri Lanka.

1880 Charles-Louis-Alphonse Laveran discovers malaria parasites in blood.

1882–1888 A French company attempts to construct a canal across Panama. The project fails, in part due to malaria.

1886 Camillo Golgi identifies two different forms of malaria.

1897 Ronald Ross finds the *Plasmodium* parasite in a mosquito's stomach.

1904	The United States begins construction of the Panama Canal. Colonel William Gorgas enacts a plan to control mosquitoes and reduce malaria at the construction site.
1947	The United States begins the National Malaria Eradication Program.
1951	Health officials report that malaria has been wiped out in the United States.
1955	The World Health Organization launches the Global Malaria Eradication Program.
1971	Scientists identify artemisinin, a malaria medication made from sweet wormwood.
1980s	*Plasmodium falciparum* begins to develop resistance to chloroquine.
1998	WHO and several other international organizations create the Roll Back Malaria Partnership.
2006	The United States holds its first White House Summit on Malaria.
2007	WHO approves the global use of DDT for indoor residual spraying in countries with widespread malaria transmission.
2008	Roll Back Malaria launches the Global Malaria Action Plan. Doctors begin to test the RTS,S malaria vaccine.
2009	The Sanaria company begins testing a new malaria vaccine.
2010	Scientists discover that King Tut, the ancient Egyptian king, died of malaria.

GLOSSARY

anemia: a condition in which a person has fewer red blood cells than normal. People with anemia do not get enough oxygen. Malaria can cause anemia.

Anopheles: the genus of mosquito that transmits human malaria. *Anopheles gambiae* carries the most dangerous form of malaria.

antibodies: proteins produced by the human immune system to fight foreign invaders such as parasites, bacteria, and viruses

artemisinin: a powerful malaria medication made from the sweet wormwood plant

bed net: mosquito nets that drape over sleeping areas to protect people from mosquito bites

cerebral malaria: a dangerous form of malaria in which damaged red blood cells clog tiny blood vessels in the brain. Cerebral malaria can cause comas, seizures, and death.

chloroquine: once the main drug used to prevent and treat malaria. Chloroquine has grown increasingly ineffective against *P. falciparum*, the most dangerous form of malaria.

Cinchona **tree:** the South American tree from which the antimalaria medication quinine was first made

DDT: (dichlorodiphenyltrichloroethane) a once-widely used insecticide. Many governments banned DDT because it harms wildlife. The World Health Organization is recommending the use of DDT in some countries because it is extremely effective against mosquitoes.

endemic: constantly present in a specific place. In places with endemic malaria, people may get malaria frequently.

epidemic: a sudden onset of an infectious disease, affecting many people in a region at the same time

host: an animal or organism within which a parasite lives. Both mosquitoes and humans are hosts to the malaria parasite.

immunity: protection generated by the body's immune system in response to foreign invaders, including bacteria, viruses, and parasites

indoor residual spraying: the practice of spraying the walls, ceilings, and roofs of houses with insecticide to kill mosquitoes that may rest there after feeding

insecticide: a chemical such as DDT that is used to kill insects

larvae: immature wingless and legless forms of insects such as mosquitoes. Mosquito larvae live in water.

larvicide: a chemical used to kill insect larvae

parasite: an organism that must live on or in another kind of organism. Parasites sometimes harm their hosts.

Plasmodium: the kind of parasite that causes malaria. Four *Plasmodium* species—*P. falciparum*, *P. malariae*, *P. ovale*, and *P. vivax*—commonly infect humans. A fifth species, *P. knowlesi*, or "monkey malaria," may become widespread among humans in the future.

quinine: a drug originally obtained from the *Cinchona* tree. Quinine was the only widely used antimalarial treatment in the world for nearly three hundred years.

red blood cells: cells within the bloodstream that carry oxygenated hemoglobin to the body. The malaria parasite spends part of its life cycle within red blood cells.

resistance: the ability of an organism to withstand certain medications or treatments. The malaria parasite has developed strains that are resistant to drugs such as chloroquine. The *Anopheles* mosquito has developed strains that are resistant to certain insecticides.

vaccine: a medication that stimulates the body to produce antibodies that fight a specific organism, usually a bacterium or virus. Scientists are testing several potential vaccines for malaria.

SOURCE NOTES

5 Terrence Smith, interview with author, March 21, 2004.

12 Fiammetta Rocco, *The Miraculous Fever-Tree: Malaria and the Quest for a Cure That Changed the World* (New York: HarperCollins Books, 2003), 32.

13 Coumba Makalou, "What It Feels Like to Have Malaria," *Nothing But Nets*, June 5, 2007, http://www.nothingbutnets.net/blogs/what-it-feels-like-to-have-malaria.html (September 24, 2009).

17 Ibid., xviii.

23 D. Morens, G. K. Folkers, and A. S. Fauci, "The Challenge of Emerging and Reemerging Infectious Diseases," *Nature* 430 (July 8, 2004): 245.

24 Naomi Mapstone, "South America: Climate Change Takes Tropical Diseases up the Mountain," Financial Times.com, April 23, 2009, http://www.ft.com/cms/s/0/80f49bd6-2ec8-11de-b7d3-00144feabdc0,dwp_uuid=f8b03b2e-2eca-11de-b7d3-00144feabdc0.html?nclick_check=1 (September 8, 2009).

28 MSF-USA Association, "Growing Insecurity Forces MSF to Leave Its Largest Health Center in Somalia," Médecins Sans Frontières, June 17, 2009, http://doctorswithoutborders.org/press/release.cfm?id=3670&cat=press-release (September 8, 2009).

34 MSF-USA Association, "In Southern Mali, MSF Improve Malaria Response," Médecins Sans Frontières, April 25, 2008, http://doctorswithoutborders.org/news/article.cfm?id=2632 (September 8, 2009).

34 Samlee Plianbangchang, "Message by Regional Director," World Health Organization Southeast Asia Region, 2004, http://w3.whosea.org/malaria/messrd.htm (March 1, 2004).

35 World Health Organization, "Drug Resistance Could Set Back Malaria Successes," Pan American Health Organization, February 25, 2009, http://new.paho.org/hq/index.php?option=com_content&task=view&id=769&Itemid=259 (September 8, 2009).

41 Smith.

42–43 *Daily Triumph*, "Hadejia Residents Blame Malaria Cases on Absense of Drainage System," August 25, 2009, http://www.triumphnewspapers.com/hades2482009.html (September 8, 2009).

44   World Health Organization, "Malaria in the Americas: No Time to Ease Up," Pan American Health Organization, November 6, 2008, http://new.paho.org/hq/index.php?option=com_content&task=view&id=393&Itemid=259 (September 8, 2009).

44–45 MSF-USA Association, "Bo, Sierra Leone: Treating Children with Malaria," Médecins Sans Frontières, April 4, 2008, http://www.doctorswithoutborders-usa.org/publications/alert/article.cfm?id=2592&cat=alert-article&ref=tag-index (September 25, 2009).

46   Save the Children Federation, "Success Story—Fighting Malaria." Save the Children, 2009, http://www.savethechildren.org/publications/success-stories/success-story-fighting-malaria.html (September 25, 2009).

47   Ibid.

47   The Global Fund to Fight AIDS, Tuberculosis and Malaria, "Fighting Malaria in the Philippines," Global Fund, 2009, http://www.theglobalfund.org/en/savinglives/philippines/malaria1/ (September 8, 2009).

48   World Health Organization, "Malaria Is Alive and Well and Killing More Than 3,000 African Children Each Day," WHO, April 25, 2003, http://www.who.int/mediacentre/news/releases/2003/pr33/en/index.html (April 6, 2009).

50   Mary McMahon, "My Story," Nurses for the Nations, 2009, http://www.nursesforthenations.org/mystory.htm (September 8, 2009).

51   Plan USA, "Togo: Teenagers Tell Stories of Malaria," Plan, 2009, https://www.planusa.org/contentmgr/showdetails.php/id/396779 (September 8, 2009).

56   Nathalie Mvondo, interview with author, August 8, 2007.

69   Michael Specter, "What Money Can Buy," *New Yorker*, October 24, 2005, 63.

89   Interview with author, Bruce Gowdy, malaria patient, August 15, 2007.

94   Katie Lewis, "Fake Drugs a Health Atrocity," *Edmonton Journal*, September 9, 2007, http://www.canada.com/edmontonjournal/news/sundayreader/story.html?id=36725e8d-9289-4ccb-9ee1-617126a8660d&p=3 (April 6, 2009).

107   *Seattle Times*, "Confronting Malaria," special report, September 23–25, 2007.

109 Bill Gates, "2009 Annual Letter from Bill Gates," Bill and Melinda Gates Foundation, 2009, http://www.gatesfoundation .org/annual-letter/Pages/2009-bill-gates-annual-letter.aspx (September 8, 2009).

111 Bill and Melinda Gates Foundation, "Major Commitment to Global Fight against Malaria," Bill and Melinda Gates Foundation, December 11, 2006, http://www.gatesfoundation .org/press-releases/Pages/malaria-control-research-advocacy-061211.aspx (April 6, 2009).

SELECTED BIBLIOGRAPHY

Centers for Disease Control and Prevention. "*Anopheles* Mosquitoes." CDC. July 30, 2008. http://www.cdc.gov/malaria/biology/mosquito/ index.htm (October 31, 2009).

———. "Frequently Asked Questions about Malaria." CDC. December 17, 2008. http://www.cdc.gov/malaria/faq.htm (October 31, 2009).

———. "The History of Malaria: An Ancient Disease." CDC. April 23, 2004. http://www.cdc.gov/malaria/history/index.htm (October 31, 2009).

———. "Malaria Parasites." CDC. April 23, 2004. http://www.cdc .gov/malaria/biology/parasites/index.htm (October 31, 2009).

———. "Schema of the Life Cycle of Malaria." CDC. February 17, 2006. http://www.cdc.gov/malaria/biology/life_cycle.htm (October 31, 2009).

Finkel, Michael. "Bedlam in the Blood: Malaria." *National Geographic* 212, no. 1 (2007): 32–67.

Helm, Kristi. "A Q&A with Bill Gates." *Seattle Times*, September 25, 2007. http://seattletimes.nwsource.com/html/localnews/2003900032_ malaraigatesfullqa.html (October 31, 2009).

McNeil, Donald G. "In the World of Life-Saving Drugs, a Growing Epidemic of Deadly Fakes." *New York Times*, February 20, 2007. http:// www.nytimes.com/2007/02/20/science/20coun .html?ex=1329627600en=ffd6f0bbe3d77a1fei=5088partner=rssnytemc= rss (October 31, 2009).

Murray, P. R., K. S. Rosenthal, and M. A. Pfaller. *Medical Microbiology.* 5th ed. Philadelphia: Elsevier, 2005.

Myser, Michael. "Hunting a Ruthless Killer." CNNMoney.com. February 7, 2006. http://money.cnn.com/magazines/business2/ business2_archive/2006/01/01/8368122/index.htm (October 31, 2009).

National Institute of Allergy and Infectious Diseases. "Malaria Research." NIAID. October 30, 2009. http://www.niaid.nih.gov/ publications/malaria2.htm (October 31, 2009).

———. "Understanding Malaria: Fighting an Ancient Scourge." NIAID. February 2007. http://www3.niaid.nih.gov/topics/Malaria/PDF/ malaria.pdf (October 31, 2009).

Path. "Malaria Vaccine." Malaria Vaccine Initiative. 2009. http://www. malariavaccine.org/malvac-overview.php (October 31, 2009).

Rocco, Fiammetta. *The Miraculous Fever-Tree: Malaria and the Quest for a Cure That Changed the World.* New York: HarperCollins Books, 2003.

Seattle Times. "Confronting Malaria." Special report, September 23–25, 2007.

Specter, Michael. "What Money Can Buy." *New Yorker,* October 24, 2005, 57–71.

World Health Organization. "Indoor Residual Spraying." WHO. 2006. http://malaria.who.int/docs/IRS-position.pdf (October 31, 2009).

———. "World Malaria Report 2008." WHO. 2008. http://malaria.who. int/wmr2008/malaria2008.pdf (October 31, 2009).

FOR FURTHER INFORMATION

Books

Abramovitz, Melissa. *Malaria*. New York: Lucent Books, 2006.

Cunningham, Kevin. *Malaria*. Greensboro, NC: Morgan Reynolds, 2009.

Fleisher, Paul. *Parasites: Latching on to a Free Lunch*. Minneapolis: Twenty-First Century Books, 2006.

Goldsmith, Connie. *Invisible Invaders: Dangerous Infectious Diseases*. Minneapolis: Twenty-First Century Books, 2006.

Marcus, Bernard A. *Malaria*. New York: Facts on File, 2004.

Naff, Clayton Farris. *Malaria*. Farmington Hills, MI: Greenhaven Press, 2009.

Films

India's War against Malaria. DVD. Washington, DC: National Archives and Records Administration, 2008.

Malaria: Fever Wars. DVD. Arlington, VA: Public Broadcasting Service, 2006.

Organizations and Websites

Bill and Melinda Gates Foundation
P.O. Box 23350
Seattle, WA 98102
(206) 709-3100
http://www.gatesfoundation.org
Bill and Melinda Gates created their foundation in 2000 because they believe that every life has equal value. Their goal is to help reduce health inequities in the United States and around the world. The organization gives a great deal of money to support malaria research, development of an effective malaria vaccine, mosquito-control projects, and the search for new drugs to treat malaria.

Centers for Disease Control and Prevention (CDC)
1600 Clifton Road
Atlanta, GA 30333
(800) 311-3435
http://www.cdc.gov/malaria
The CDC's mission is to promote health and quality of life by preventing and controlling disease, injury, and disability. The CDC monitors and investigates health problems around the world and in the United States. Its website offers extensive information about malaria. It also offers health recommendations for travelers to foreign countries.

Global Malaria Programme (GMP)
http://www.who.int/malaria
The Global Malaria Programme is part of the World Health Organization (WHO), the foremost global authority on health. GMP is responsible for malaria surveillance, monitoring, and evaluation; policy and strategy formulation; technical assistance; and coordination of WHO's global efforts to fight malaria.

London School of Hygiene and Tropical Medicine
Keppel Street
London WC1E 7HT
http://www.lshtm.ac.uk
The London School of Hygiene and Tropical Medicine is Britain's national school of public health and the world's leading center for malaria research.

Malaria No More
432 Park Avenue South, 13th Floor
New York, NY 10016
(212) 792-7929
http://www.malarianomore.org
The organization's mission is to end deaths due to malaria. It works to provide bed nets, medication, indoor insecticide spraying, and education to families in need. The group formed in 2006 and works in partnership with the President's Malaria Initiative, UNICEF, the American Red Cross, and several other groups.

Malaria Vaccine Initiative (MVI)
 7500 Old Georgetown Road, Suite 1200
 Bethesda, MD 20814
 (240) 395-2700
 http://www.malariavaccine.org
 The MVI's mission is to speed up the development of promising
 malaria vaccines and to ensure their availability and accessibility in the
 developing world. The site provides information on vaccines that are
 being tested and lists the global partners involved in vaccine projects.

Medicines for Malaria Venture (MMV)
 P.O. Box 1826
 1215 Geneva 15
 Switzerland
 41 22 799 4060
 http://www.mmv.org
 The MMV is a nonprofit organization created to discover, develop,
 and deliver new antimalarial drugs through effective public–private
 partnerships. The organization brings public, private, and charitable
 partners together to fund and manage the discovery, development, and
 registration of new medicines to prevent and treat malaria in countries
 where the disease is endemic.

National Institute of Allergy and Infectious Diseases
 6610 Rockledge Drive, MSC 6612
 Bethesda, MD 20892-6612
 (301) 402-1663
 http://www.niaid.nih.gov
 This organization is part of the prestigious National Institutes of
 Health. Click on the website's "Health & Research Topics" to find
 information about malaria. That section has detailed information on
 malaria, malaria research, and the human immune system.

Nothing But Nets
P.O. Box 96539
Washington, DC 20090-6539
(202) 887-9040
http://www.nothingbutnets.net
This organization is a global, grassroots campaign to fight malaria
in Africa by delivering insecticide-treated bed nets to families with
children. Each ten-dollar donation goes directly toward the purchase
and delivery of nets. The Bill and Melinda Gates Foundation matches
each donated net with a second net.

Roll Back Malaria
http://www.rbm.who.int
Roll Back Malaria is an international partnership made up of the World
Health Organization, UNICEF, the World Bank, and others. Its mission
is to provide a coordinated global approach to fighting malaria. Goals are
to decrease the malaria death rate, decrease the number of malaria cases,
increase the number of households with insecticide-treated bed nets, and
increase the number of patients who receive treatment within twenty-
four hours of experiencing symptoms. The website provides extensive
information on malaria, including detailed reports on the status of
malaria in many nations.

UNICEF
http://www.unicef.org
Part of the United Nations, UNICEF works to build a world in which
every child receives health care, education, protection, and equality.
Go to the site and search for malaria to see how this disease affects
children around the world.

INDEX

Photo Acknowledgments

The images in this book are used with the permission of: © LSHTM/ Photo Researchers, Inc., p. 1; © Mikkel Ostergaard/Panos Pictures, p. 4; Centers for Disease Control and Prevention Public Health Image Library/ Jim Gathany, p. 6; © age fotostock/SuperStock, pp. 8–9; © Marc Deville/ Getty Images, p. 10; © SuperStock/SuperStock, p. 12; © W. Beloi/Henry Guttmann/Hulton Archive/Getty Images, p. 15; © Interfoto/Alamy, p. 16 (top); © Hulton Archive/Getty Images, p. 16 (bottom); Library of Congress, p. 19 (LC-USZ62-125807); © Michael Hall/Photonica/Getty Images, pp. 22–23; © Jason Edwards/National Geographic/Getty Images, p. 25; © Peter Barritt/SuperStock, pp. 26–27; © Peeter Viisimaa/iStock Exclusive/Getty Images, pp. 30–31; © Laura Westlund/Independent Picture Service, pp. 33, 34–35, 38, 62–63; © Giacomo Pirozzi/Panos Pictures, pp. 40–41, 74, 96; © Scott Dalton/Bloomberg via Getty Images, p. 42; © Caroline Penn/Panos Pictures, p. 45; © Paula Bronstein/Getty Images, p. 49; Centers for Disease Control and Prevention Public Health Image Library/James D. Gathany, pp. 52–53; AP Photo/Marianne Armshaw, p. 54; Centers for Disease Control and Prevention Public Health Image Library/Dr. William Collins, p. 57; Centers for Disease Control and Prevention Public Health Image Library/Steven Glenn, Laboratory & Consultation Division, p. 59; © Alexander Joe/AFP/Getty Images, pp. 66–67; © Mario Villafuerte/Getty Images, p. 68; © David McLain/ Aurora/Getty Images, p. 71; Centers for Disease Control and Prevention Public Health Image Library/B. Partin, Jimmy Stewart, p. 77; © William Daniels/Panos Pictures, pp. 80–81; Centers for Disease Control and Prevention Public Health Image Library, p. 85; © Jenny Matthews/Panos Pictures, p. 86; © Sven Torfinn/Panos Pictures, p. 90; Sipa via AP Photo, p. 98; © Tim Sloan/AFP/Getty Images, p. 105; AP Photo/Elaine Thompson, p. 107; © Marcus Rose/Panos Pictures, p. 108; © Peter Barker/ Panos Pictures, pp. 110–111.

Front cover: © Thomas Holton/The Image Bank/Getty Images (main); © LSHTM/Photo Researchers, Inc. (title type).

About the Author

Connie Goldsmith is a registered nurse with a bachelor of science degree in nursing and a master of public administration degree in health care. In addition to writing several nonfiction books for middle-school and upper-grade readers, Goldsmith has also published more than two hundred magazine articles, mostly on health topics for adults and children. She writes a children's book review column for a regional parenting magazine in Sacramento, California, where she lives.